# Writing through the Darkness

Hi Patt & Steve,

John & I really enjoyed your company at Yvonne & Ron's home recently! As promised, here's a copy of my book ... hope you'll enjoy it.

Warmly,
Beth

Elizabeth Maynard Schaefer
29902 Sugar Maple Court
Hayward, CA 94544

*To Patt & Steve*
*With warm wishes for*
*joyful creative endeavors*
*Beth*

# Writing through the Darkness

*easing your depression with*
*paper and pen*

*Elizabeth Maynard Schaefer, Ph.D.*

**CELESTIAL ARTS**
**Berkeley | Toronto**

Disclaimer: This book and its contents are for informational purposes only. It is not intended to
be a substitute for treatment by or the advice and care of a professional health care provider. While
the author and publisher have endeavored to ensure that the information presented is factual, no
warranty is provided nor results guaranteed.

Celestial Arts
an imprint of Ten Speed Press
PO Box 7123
Berkeley, California 94707
www.tenspeed.com

Distributed in Australia by Simon and Schuster Australia, in Canada by Ten Speed Press Canada,
in New Zealand by Southern Publishers Group, in South Africa by Real Books, and in the United
Kingdom and Europe by Publishers Group UK.

Cover and text design by Nancy Austin

Excerpts appearing in Another Voice sections have been used with permission from the authors.

Library of Congress Cataloging-in-Publication Data
Schaefer, Elizabeth Maynard.
  Writing through the darkness : easing your depression with paper and pen /
Elizabeth Maynard Schaefer.
       p. cm.
  Summary: "A guide to using creative writing methods to ease the symptoms of depression,
from the founder of a creative writing course for people with mood disorders"—Provided by
publisher.
  Includes bibliographical references and index.
  ISBN-13: 978-1-58761-319-7
  ISBN-10: 1-58761-319-0
  1. Depression, Mental—Treatment 2. Creative writing—Thearapeutic use.
I. Title.
  RC537.S382 2008
  616.89'165—dc22

                              2007050244

Printed in the United States of America
First printing, 2008

1 2 3 4 5 6 7 8 9 10 — 12 11 10 09 08

*Dedicated to all those brave enough to write while living with depression, including the warm and generous members of my writing group at Stanford, past and present.*

# Contents

# Acknowledgments

My deepest gratitude goes to all those who have helped and supported me through my health challenges and through the creation of this book. In particular, I thank my agent, Elise Proulx, for her immediate excitement about this project and for finding it a good home; my editor at Celestial Arts, Julie Bennett, for her kind and professional nurturance of this project from proposal to completed book, and all the other fine members of "the team" at Celestial, for their enthusiasm and professionalism; the Stanford University Department of Psychiatry and Behavioral Sciences, for providing a home for the last ten years for the creative writing group for people with mood disorders; John Barry, M.D., for twenty-plus years of steadfast encouragement and the best health care I could ask for; Brent Solvason, M.D., for kindly providing some of the treatments key to my good health these last few years; Carolyn Foster, for direction and wonderful inspiration; Eric Greenleaf, for generous support and perspective; my fabulous long-standing Wednesday night writing circle: Zoe Carter, Gina DePaulo, Nelle Engoron, and Connie Hanstedt, for both positive and helpful feedback; Kathleen Chambers, for friendship, feedback, and common sense; Katherine Lerer, for friendship, unending encouragement, and camaraderie; my brother, Mark Maynard, D.O.M., for teaching me to live gracefully with ill health; my late father, Charles W. Maynard, Ph.D., for showing me what fun it can be to explore a new field; my mother, Joan M. Maynard, for love, support, and friendship in the tough times and the good times—and for encouraging me for years to write this down; and my husband, John W. Schaefer, my best friend, my first editor of everything, the love of my life, and the reason I'm here today.

# Introduction: Writing Really *Can* Help Depression

*Writing is medicine. It is an appropriate antidote to injury.*
*It is an appropriate companion for any difficult change.*

—Julia Cameron, *The Right to Write*

It's Tuesday afternoon. Around a conference room table in Stanford University's Psychiatry and Behavioral Sciences building, twelve people are chatting as they take their seats. An attorney, two teachers, a physician, a saleswoman, a graphic artist, a realtor, two engineers, an acupuncturist, and a couple of college students—all are coping with profound depression or problematic bipolar disorder. Women and men from across the San Francisco Bay Area, they range in age from twenty-two to seventy-five. Most are on mental health disability from their jobs; some work or volunteer part time; a few are beginning to job hunt after a considerable period of illness.

They have found their way here from fliers I've placed in the psychiatry clinic, from friends and support groups, or they have been referred by mental health care professionals. Some already write frequently in journals; a few are visual artists as well. They are looking for social support as they delve into their lives and their depression in a creative way. They have gathered, as they do every week, for this group, simply advertised as "Creative Writing for People with Mood Disorders."

"This class is the most important part of my week—more important than my psychiatrist appointment or my psychotherapy," declares one student as we pull out pens and open notebooks. For a person with severe depression, that's saying a lot, and I smile my thanks to her. Then we jump right in; talking will come later in the two-hour session.

"Let's start with something concrete to warm up with—and remember the most important rule: write continuously; you don't need to stop to think or correct yourself. Now, describe your childhood bedroom. What did it look like? What did you do there? What stories do you recall? Let's write for ten minutes." Heads bow and hands move steadily across the pages of spiral notebooks and decorated journals.

Absorbed in creating my own narrative, it is only when I glance up to check the clock that my eyes fall on curly headed Patti quickly scribbling, her nose just inches from the page. She recently spent two solid years in bed, depressed and terrified of leaving her home. Beside her sits Wayne. Though his usually cheerful demeanor in this class might not suggest it, he has required many treatments with electroconvulsive therapy for his depression this year. Now he is unable to work at the career he loved because the treatments have erased the detailed memories his job demanded. On his other side is slim Anita, wearing long colorful earrings. She wrote last week about recently spending hours on the Golden Gate Bridge, contemplating a quick plunge to her death to end her decades of anguishing moods.

I admire these people tremendously. Not content to rely solely on traditional medical treatments, they are here to work hard exploring their thoughts, feelings, and beliefs, including traumas that may have shaped their pasts, and the toll depression has taken on their lives. They are here to create, putting one word after another to tell stories only they can tell. And they are here to support and help each other by sharing their own writing and accepting without judgment what their peers offer. All of us believe that being here is taking a step toward wellness.

* * * *

*Writing through the Darkness* is designed to show you, a person coping with depression, how to start on your own healing voyage by making writing a part of your treatment regimen. It is an introduction to how and why writing can ease your depression, as well as a guide to get you writing in ways that are healing for *you*, whether you write on your own or in a group. I've

2

written for eighteen years—as a journalist, scientist, poet, memoirist, and blogger, and for personal growth and healing from deep depression. And for ten years I've assisted others who have depression on their writing and healing quests. In that time I've learned a great deal about what seems to help heal, what doesn't, and what can even hurt.

Lots of exciting evidence demonstrates how writing can be therapeutic in many ways. "It reduces the physical and mental stress involved in inhibiting thoughts," says Dr. James Pennebaker, professor of psychology, now at the University of Texas at Austin. "But more importantly, writing is a powerful tool to organize overwhelming events and make them manageable. . . . Once organized, they are easier to resolve."[1]

I want you to begin right away to feel the excitement, relief, insight, calm, and joy that writing offers, so chapter 1 of *Writing through the Darkness* tells you exactly how to start today, including the (very minimal) equipment you'll need and the three writing "rules" to follow. It offers a list of possible writing topics and approaches specific to you, a writer with depression. And it answers that nagging question, "But how can I write when I'm depressed?" with ideas and techniques to spur you on.

In later chapters of part I you'll learn much more about the writing-depression connection, including how writing can bolster your health, your emotions, even your spiritual life. In part II, you'll learn a variety of techniques for exploring different types of writing, and I'll discuss sharing your writing with others. You'll also get lots more ideas about how to write by *using* your depression, rather than fighting against it. In part III, you'll find out how a writing group for people with depression can lead writers to heal in a safe community, and you'll discover practical information about how you can start a group, and where to go next with your writing.

Throughout *Writing through the Darkness*, you'll discover many writing topics and exercises to try out as you read. These are designed to jump-start your creative mind as they lead you to the types of writing you most enjoy exploring and find most healing. Many examples of writing by members of my writing group are included. Mixed in are comments from well-known authors, which have provided encouragement and inspiration to me. I believe you'll find writing to ease your depression an amazing adventure— sometimes calming and soothing, sometimes stirring, sometimes sad, and sometimes joyful. You're already making a significant move toward your recovery from depression by picking up this book and considering a new, adjunct treatment.

Note: Persons who have contributed writing samples for this book have provided explicit permission for their work to be printed here. When only a first name is used on a writing sample, it is to be assumed that this is a pseudonym. In the text, identifying characteristics of writing group members have been changed to protect their identities.

# I.
# THE WRITING–DEPRESSION CONNECTION

# Chapter I

# Start Writing and Healing Today

*Give sorrow words; the grief that does not
Speak
Whispers the oe'r fraught heart and bids it
Break.*

—William Shakespeare, *Macbeth*

I lay limp on a bed in a simple cinderblock room, waiting for more shock treatments, wishing I could roll over and die right there, right then. I was scarcely able to imagine any life after this week's grim stay on the hospital's locked ward. All the pills I was swallowing every few hours were doing nothing, I was sure. Even the electroconvulsive therapy I was receiving every other day, which had worked wonders for me in the past, seemed futile this time. Desperate, I reached for an empty notebook. My brain was too flat and blurred to put together sentences, so I scribbled a list of words about my situation and slammed the book shut. Immediately I felt some lifting of the black cloud of a depression so bleak that it scrambled my thoughts and choked my breath.

\* \* \* \*

I remember the first time a doctor suggested I take an antidepressant medication. I was at the Stanford University student health center. "Who, me? Depressed?" I thought with alarm. "And taking pills for it? *I'm* well adjusted; *I* certainly don't need medicine to be happy!" Still, I had been crying, apathetic, and exhausted for weeks. So, fearing I was on a slippery slope toward "crazy," I reluctantly agreed to the daily pills.

That day, as I trudged slowly across campus, back to the biology lab where I worked on research toward my Ph.D., I wracked my confused mind about what could be going on. I had thought I was happy. I had grown up in a family who loved me, and showed it. I had never been abused, didn't use drugs. I was excited about graduate school, and I was delighted that less than a year ago I had married John, my blond, always-smiling college sweetheart, just two weeks after we graduated. We had looked forward with excitement to this new life in Northern California where we were headed a week later.

All seemed fine as I scanned my life, looking for reasons to be depressed. However, I had to admit I'd had a lot of major changes in my life in the last year. And, as every Psychology 101 student learns, stress, whether from good things or bad things, is still stress. Maybe, I pondered, I had been under enough stress to trigger this sorrowful exhaustion that was beginning to feel hopeless. Just a few months later, I became grateful that I had followed the doctor's advice—to my tremendous relief, the depression lifted.

By the end of graduate school, four years later, I had been on and off of antidepressants half a dozen times. I was ruminating about my future, too. Did I want to continue on my original career path as a scientist or pursue the science journalism I had started doing on the side? As I reflected on how I loved talking to scientists, engineers, and physicians about their research and how, as I had since childhood, I loved the writing process itself, I made my decision: science writing it would be.

I spent my last few months of graduate school happily working part time on the side at my exciting new job as the West Coast correspondent for the English science journal *Nature*. But a few months after leaving campus with my diploma, I found myself tired and anxious and then sad for no obvious reason. Suddenly it became nearly impossible to pick up the phone to call on the scientists I needed to interview. As I began to fear, my despair soon returned, and this time it quickly grew much deeper than ever before.

I started taking the new, much-heralded Prozac. But six days later I cut my wrist and forearm in an effort to release my pain and found myself on the hospital's locked psychiatric ward for the first of several stays. After a week of answering questions from doctors and beginning the adjustment to two new medicines, I was released. Still feeling sad and lost, I was at least calmer. But something else happened that week, too: I started writing a few lines in a journal now and then, something I'd played with sometimes at other difficult junctures in life.

At home, still physically weak from the new meds and emotionally fragile, I sat cross-legged on the sofa and wrote for hours a day, not knowing what else to do with myself as I tried to recover. I used my words to try to puzzle out my situation logically, and I recorded every memory I could think of, good, bad, and otherwise, without knowing why. Filling pages was my one sure accomplishment each day. However, I could not imagine myself in a professional position again. Within weeks, I sadly tendered my job resignation, doubting that my now-unreliable mind could ever work again.

As seasons passed, I wrote daily, often about my mental health, which came and went frequently. Meanwhile some new and bizarre phenomena surfaced: several antidepressants we tried caused my thoughts to race crazily so that some days I was elated about grandiose plans of writing a complete screenplay and running a marathon all before dinnertime. Soon I had a new label: I had bipolar disorder, formerly known as manic depression, a condition in which moods swing unpredictably between manic highs and the depressed lows I knew too well. I also began to hear voices when I was alone and to catch glimpses of strangers and animals when I entered a room.

After trying twenty-plus medications, we turned to something I thought only "other" depressed people got—people in much worse shape than I could ever be: electroconvulsive therapy (ECT), commonly known as shock treatments. Scary though it sounded at first, ECT was my savior. Two weeks and six treatments later, I had my personality back. The repeated seizures had somehow reset my brain's chemistry, and I was a new woman. No, I was my old self.

For most of my thirties I needed ECT every few months, along with taking my cocktail of medicines. But I kept writing, too—recording the ride between happiness and the ever-circling doom. When I could, I began to develop my journaling into other forms, creating stories and poems. Then, echoing my own tentative thoughts, my psychiatrist suggested I write a book to help slay the depression that now sometimes appeared as a menacing serpent in my dreams. I began the long, slow process of writing a memoir of my illness.

Eventually I began to come to terms with my up-and-down situation and to want more out of the life I had. Between relapses, I joined a women's writing group where we supported and critiqued each other's work, I edited several books, and I took writing workshops and classes whenever I could. And I realized that this was potent medicine for me too, helping my emotions to stabilize and my thoughts to clear. As my confidence grew I became certain that I'd keep writing in this personal way. Writing was as healing to me as all my medical treatments—this *did* matter. Writing helped bring me back. Writing saved my life.

## Sharing the Writing Treasure with Others

In 1998, I proposed an idea that had been percolating in me for a long time: I would offer to lead a creative writing group for other people with mood disorders at Stanford. I suggested it to the leader of a depression support group I had discovered and to a creativity researcher in the bipolar clinic, and they jumped at the idea. Encouraged too by my psychiatrist, I posted fliers to recruit fellow depressed persons and began drawing up lesson plans. Soon a handful of us were meeting weekly to write together, read our pieces aloud, and talk about how this method of exploring our illnesses and our feelings gave us insight and relief.

I was thrilled. Here I could share all I'd learned about writing from innumerable books, classes, groups, and years of writing—something that had now become one of my buttresses—and try to help others who were on their own path through the depths of depression and bipolar disorder. I taught them of the scientific evidence that was appearing about how writing can best help you heal from traumas and how it is being used for many groups, whether sick, traumatized, or healthy. I provided topics, both about depression and about other issues, and we wrote memories, poems, stories, ideas, thoughts, and deepest feelings and read them to each other. Reactions I had never anticipated were triggered in me at times as I wrote, and in the others, too. Best of all, we supported each other as kin who had this special, life-altering experience of depression in common. It boosted my self-esteem, and it kept me feeling that I still was, indeed, a writer. The class continued to grow and became the highlight of my week.

After ten years, the writing group at Stanford for people with mood disorders is going stronger than ever. Writers travel from all over the San Francisco Bay Area to attend. Scores, maybe hundreds, of writers coping with depression have taken part, sometimes for years. These people continue to awe me with their brave words about tragic experiences and excruciating illnesses, and with their determined steps toward building new, healthier lives. They encouraged me to write this book, to share more broadly the ideas and techniques that have helped us dig deep as well as helped lift us up. I offer it with the hope that its words—and *your* words—will be healing to you.

## How to Use This Book

*Writing through the Darkness* is organized into three parts, which you can use in whichever order you like. After you get started writing in this chapter, you can continue through the rest of part I, *The Writing-Depression Connection*, to learn about the myriad relationships between writing and depression. Here we'll look at what depression is and what can be done to treat it, even when the stigma that surrounds it is an issue. Then we'll examine the question of whether writing is "therapy" for depression and we'll look at how writing has been used by depressed authors in various periods. We'll also consider the many powerful ways in which writing can help you—

through your body, as fascinating research proves, and through your mind, heart, and spirit.

*But,* if you're eager to just keep writing at the moment, go ahead and jump to part II of the book. And if you're a writing veteran who's especially interested in groups for people with depression, turn to part III.

In part II, *Write It Out: How to Write through the Darkness,* you'll learn the nitty-gritty of writing to ease depression. You'll start with the fundamentals—journaling and freewriting—as you develop a regular writing habit. Then you'll explore writing poetry, memoir, fiction, and even writing for others through speeches and publication. Tasting from this menu of writing genres and techniques will help you discover what types of writing you most enjoy and find most healing.

In part III, *Where to Go from Here,* you'll learn how to take your writing further. We'll discuss how healing from depression can take place in a group setting, and you'll learn how you can develop your own writing group for people with depression. In addition, you'll discover ideas and encouragement to help you continue writing, whether on your own or in a group—including lots of stimulating exercise ideas.

## All You Need: Simple Tools and a Little Time

One of the wonderful things about writing is that you don't need a lot of equipment or preparation to do it. You don't need any special degrees or previous writing experience to benefit from it. All you need are a pen and a notebook, or a computer, a comfortable spot in which to sit, and a bit of time carved out of your schedule.

First, let's discuss the pen (actually, the pens: always have an extra one for those times when you're having an epiphany and you run out of ink). For some people, this writing tool is very important; for others, whatever they picked up at the bank will do. If you like, find yourself an antique fountain pen or a fancy gold ballpoint or a gel-writer in the perfect shade. Personally, colors intrigue me and even comfort me when I'm low, so I have several extra-fine rolling balls in about five colors on my desk. And in my purse . . . and by the phone. . . . I'm a little compulsive about this. They're inexpensive and last a long time, and I get to choose a color according to my mood. Whatever you use, whether it's a carefully guarded favorite or just what you keep around the house, the only real requirement is that it doesn't impede you as you put down your fast and continuous thoughts. So make sure that it writes quickly and smoothly.

Next, you'll need something to write on. I suggest using some sort of notebook or journal, rather than loose pages, so that you can keep things together and in chronological order in case you want to look back at your work later. It doesn't matter what kind of book or notebook you use. People have kindly given me some beautiful blank books over the years. I tend to alternate these with sixty-nine-cent steno pads I get on sale at back-to-school time. Somehow, filling one book and then cracking open a new one of a completely different ilk keeps my outlook fresher—while I love the elegant satin-covered ones, sometimes I feel freer when I write in the cheapies. Whatever you choose, use that notebook exclusively for your own writing in order to honor its importance.

"But what about my computer?" you may be asking. Yes, it's fine to write on your computer. Some people much prefer it, find it faster, and can easily schedule writing time into a day already spent in front of the screen for other reasons. I do recommend, however, that you give writing by hand a try too, and compare the feel of it with typing. Writing with paper and pen puts you in more direct physical contact with your words; I feel this leads me to access a more creative part of myself. In addition, you may find that your writing voice is slightly different with these two techniques. I also know writers who, for example, write on the computer except when composing poetry, when they feel a slower pace and the more tactile quality of paper is desirable. There's no right or wrong answer, so play and see what works best for you.

The other key issues to consider as you begin writing include *where* and *when* you will write. (For now, we'll assume you are writing at your leisure—in chapter 6, *Journaling and Freewriting as You Build Your Writing Habit*, we'll discuss how and why to develop a frequent writing habit.) Again, you'll probably need to experiment a bit with different times and places to see what you like. You'll need to be free of people demanding things of you, either in person or by phone. However, that doesn't necessarily mean you need complete silence. While some writers find that the quiet kitchen table with a cup of tea is the only way to go, others, like me, are comfortably able to tune out other patrons' conversations in a coffee house and actually prefer the stimulation of having people around. Depending on your life, you may need to write before the kids get up or after roommates go to bed or to spend lunchtime at the office writing. In addition, those of us coping with depression need to be aware of our internal rhythms. For example, sometimes I'm so drowsy that I function very poorly in the morning, so afternoon is my best writing time.

Some writers feel that ritual is an important aspect of their writing process too, that certain details can help communicate to their unconscious mind that it's writing time. You can consider what encourages you to actually pick up that pen and put your seat on that chair instead of just thinking about it. For example, is writing the very first thing in the morning the most clarifying and fulfilling for you? Are you more able to focus when you curl up on the same sofa every time? Does it help to light a candle, repeat a mantra, say a prayer, or do some other ritual to set the mood for your creative mind to come out and play? Again, experiment and use your intuition to find what feels right for you.

## *Start with Just Three Simple Rules*

Three "rules" are the most important when I lead writing groups, and I use them when creating first drafts of my own projects as well. The first is one basic to the freewriting techniques taught by writers for years: **write continuously**.

For the "To Write" exercises in this book, I'd like you to write for ten or twenty minutes (you decide which ahead of time) and—here's the kicker—you need to write the whole time and not stop. This sounds scary at first because it is not the way we were taught in school, where we thought out every word before putting it down in our essay exams. But when you keep writing no matter what, you tend to access the more creative, more emotionally insightful parts of your brain rather than your picky "editor brain," which likes to criticize what you're doing. If you get to a point where you don't know what to say next, just repeat what you've already written or simply write over and over, "I don't know what to say. I don't know what to say. . . ." This is very boring, so your mind soon comes up with something to say.

The second rule I like to emphasize is: **write this for *you*.** Unless you specifically *choose* to share it, no one else will ever know what you've put down. So don't bother to feel self-conscious about your words and don't feel they need to be perfect. Don't worry about punctuation, spelling, grammar, or constructing a careful argument. If sentences don't seem to come, go ahead and write the phrases or words that come to mind. No one is grading this. Also, as you begin to experiment with writing, don't be too concerned about needing to use

*What people somehow (inadvertently, I'm sure) forgot to mention when we were children was that we need to make messes in order to find out who we are and why we are here—and, by extension, what we're supposed to be writing.*

—ANNE LAMOTT, *Bird by Bird*

a certain style; your own unique style, or writer's voice, will develop and evolve over time.

What you write about is also ultimately up to you. In my groups, and in my own poems and stories, we write both about issues surrounding our depression (What one action helps you most to get through the day?) and seemingly unrelated issues (Who was your childhood hero?). However, if you feel compelled to write on another particular topic at any time, do it. You can always go where your writing draws you, and it is usually important to listen to your writing mind and do this—it knows what you need to explore and heal from better than anyone else. Also, if you begin writing on an assigned topic and find yourself shifting to another one midstream, this is fine. You are probably approaching something valuable.

This leads to the third very important rule: **if something feels too threatening, don't write on it.** If you feel that writing on a particular topic at a particular time is more than you can emotionally handle, don't do it. You'll gradually learn to explore and safely challenge yourself in your writing. To facilitate this, I often provide an alternate topic suggestion in my group when we are writing on an especially emotional issue. Stay aware of your feelings, and if a subject is beyond what feels healthy for you right now, be smart and shift to something else. It may be a great topic for you next month or next year, or after talking with your mental health care provider.

After writing on a topic that leaves you very emotional, it's a good idea to come back to the world gradually by writing for ten minutes or so on something positive or at least a bit less provocative, or by sharing and discussing your work with peers if you're writing in a group. Research shows that it's not uncommon to feel sad for an hour or so after writing about something emotionally difficult but that then writers typically feel better than before they wrote.[1] Overall, be attentive to your feelings and be kind to yourself as you write and afterward.

Two questions commonly come up at this point for people new to writing to ease depression: What makes writing different for people with depression? And can I really do this when I'm depressed? Let's look briefly at both issues.

## Writing Is Different for People with Depression

All writers have times of struggle with their craft, uncertainty about their topic matter, doubts about their work, or fear of how it will be received. But people writing to ease their depression may also have special issues and concerns about their subject matter and the way they approach it.

For example, you will have some unique topics to investigate because you have experienced depression. The writing prompts in this book will include some that are directly related to your depression experience and some that are not—or not obviously. Among those depression subjects, you may discover that you want to explore some of the following:

- Events occurring just before your illness

- Your family history of depression

- How your symptoms feel

- Whether you've shared your depression with others and how it has been received

- How depression has affected your work life

- How depression has affected your home life

- How depression has affected your important relationships

- Seeking help

- Getting treatment and how you feel about psychotherapy, medicines, or other treatments

- The societal stigma surrounding depression

- How your condition is changing over time

- How you will plan and work toward your recovery

- How the experience of depression will affect you in the future

That list might look intimidating, and it's true that some of these subjects will probably evoke strong emotions in you. So we'll start very slowly. Keep in mind that you'll be writing on all types of topics—a walk in the woods or a favorite childhood toy, for example—not just depression. And you'll see that issues other than your mental health may be fertile ground for healing in less direct ways.

You should also trust your own instincts on when and how to proceed with various subjects. For example, if a particular dream or relationship or image comes up often in your writing or has a real spark to it, it may be something you need to delve into in order to heal. Conversely, if a particular memory is haunting you in a frightening way, you'll want to carefully consider when and how you approach it in your writing. Keep in mind that this is a gradual process. You'll soon learn how to push yourself, but not too much. Also keep in mind that every human being, depressed or not, has issues. In many workshops and classes, I've seen again and again what a powerful means of self-expression writing can be for *everyone*.

*Writing about my mental health (or lack thereof) helps me to make sense of it and my anger and confusion associated with it.*

—ANNA

This book and its approach to writing and healing are designed specifically for people coping with situational depressions due to a difficult life event, or with major depression, or the depressed phase of bipolar disorder. It may also be useful to people with other mental health conditions. Whoever you are, whatever your situation, you'll have writing topics to investigate that are shared by everyone and those that are unique.

## But How Can You Write When You're Depressed?

Are you dubious about being able to write because of the state you're in— even though you'd like to give it a try? Remember, as anyone who's been there knows, in depression everything looks extremely serious: a partner's casual remark seems to threaten the relationship, forgetting to pick up milk at the store proves you are the "dummy" you feared, and so on. If you want to write, try not to be too serious about it. That is, don't make it another chore in your life. Writing can lift you, comfort you, and amaze you at times—it may become the best part of your day.

If you're at all able, push yourself to sit down and get started. You don't need to be in an inspired mood to write. Nearly all professional writers require themselves to complete their daily hours or pages of writing, no matter what their state of mind. All you have to do is begin—write one word, one sentence, one idea. And then it will likely start to flow. You'll forget about your present pain or lethargy and you'll begin to be caught up in this world you're describing and creating. If you've ever practiced a musical instrument, been a runner, or done a homework assignment, you already know that there are days when you just don't want to face your task. But you also know how to overcome your weariness: just begin, and it soon gets much, much easier.

If you're in a severe depression, it may be very tough to reach out for that pen on the desk—but it is possible. I've written while hospitalized with depression, as described earlier, and found that putting down even a few words granted me a small sense of power. A member of my writing group, Sandra, struggled with an extreme depression that left her literally in bed for years. When she was able to tentatively venture out, she discovered writing, and she swore she'd never, ever stop. Even on days she could only write in bed, it helped her to steady and even appreciate her life. She is now much healthier and is job hunting.

No matter what your mood is, rather than considering writing to be a formidable task, look at it as a form of release. Make that notebook or computer your friend. Accept that whatever you can put down is valid and important and will not be judged but will open your aching heart and mind, bit by bit, or even in a rush. On those days when all you can do is describe the weather or report what you ate for breakfast, feel a sense of accomplishment even for that—you did something positive by filling a page with words. This is important—it is the beginning of developing momentum, of making writing a regular habit so that it will be most healing for you. It

> *Writing . . . has been a sturdy ladder out of a deep pit.*
>
> —Alice Walker

is even an opportunity to take charge of your own recovery from depression by embracing your life and seeking to understand it. And never, ever forget that you may just find writing fun!

This book offers lots of suggestions for exercises to get you moving as well as tips on ways to approach writing, even when your mood is low. If one thing doesn't work well for you, just grab another and go. Make a small effort, and the rewards can be great. Just get started. Go.

## An Important Note of Warning

Writing is powerful, exciting, eye-opening, and healing, but it is *not* intended to be used in place of treatments recommended by your physician or psychotherapist. Don't change your treatment plan without consulting your mental health care professional; instead, use writing as an adjunct technique. If you feel you are in crisis, there is contact information for a national depression hotline in the *Bibliography and Selected Resources* section at the back of this book.

### to write

#### YOUR CHILDHOOD KITCHEN

You don't need to start writing about huge issues like freedom or the history of the world. Instead, start with a more concrete topic and really explore it.

Describe the kitchen in your childhood home. Consider, for example, what the refrigerator looked like. Was there linoleum on the floor? Were there always dirty dishes on the counter, or did every surface shine? Who cooked there, and what else went on in that room?

#### GRATITUDE

Next, using the same kind of specific descriptions, let's take on a broader subject: what are you grateful for? Remember, you can go in any direction you want—just write continuously.

Here's a portion of what a member of my writing group wrote on this topic.

## *Gratitude* by Kerwin J. Lee, M.D.

What does gratitude mean to me? It is thanks for the cold mountain stream that quenches my thirst, thanks for a walk through a quiet forest with a hint of a cooling breeze. It is thanks that there are people that uplift me. I am grateful for life. I am grateful that I survive all of the challenges in my life. Of course I do not do this without all who uplift me. It is odd how different life looks when I think of my dreams of despair versus the good people in my life.

# Chapter 2

# Getting Our Terms Straight: Depression, Therapy, and Art

*Illness of the mind is real illness. . . . As organs go, the brain is quite an important one, and its malfunctions should be addressed accordingly.*

—ANDREW SOLOMON, *The Noonday Demon*

When a friend told me recently that he was "so depressed" because his favorite football team had lost a big game, I clenched my teeth. I knew what he meant and knew that in fact he would only be disheartened and frustrated for a day or so. I'm defensive about this word "depression" and the way we sometimes throw it around so lightly.

Virtually everyone has either felt the pain of major depression or knows someone who has. In the United States, nearly twenty-one million adults (9.5 percent of the adult population) have a mood disorder in any given year.[1] And the numbers get even worse. Think of your four closest friends: odds are at least one of the five of you will suffer a depression during your lifetime.[2] The illness of depression has been recognized, described, and studied since at least the times of the ancient Greeks. In modern times, many people became aware of depression's prevalence in the early 1990s when the antidepressant drug Prozac was introduced and made national magazine covers and news reports.

Since you're holding this book, I suspect you've experienced a serious depression in one of its many guises: a *situational depression* caused by a difficult life event such as a divorce, job loss, or loss of a loved one; or a medical illness known as a *mood disorder*, which could be major depression, dysthymia (chronic mild depression), or bipolar disorder (an illness involving alternating periods of depression and overactive mania or, less severe, hypomania).

Discussions in this book will focus on mood disorders, but the writing processes you'll learn about here are just as useful if you're coping with a situational depression. Writing can help you overcome the trauma of a situational depression more quickly and assist you in finding perspective on how this event fits into your whole life. You've felt the pain of a serious depression, but you may not be aware of all of its potential health effects or its toll on society. Let's examine the facts and then consider how writing can help.

## The Seriousness of Depression

Depression is a brain disorder—it is not a character flaw. It is a treatable medical illness marked by changes in mood, thoughts, energy, and behavior, and it is the most common mental illness in the United States.

Depression can be diagnosed if five or more of the following symptoms occur each day during a two-week period or if symptoms interfere with work or family activities:[3]

- Prolonged sadness or unexplained crying spells

- Significant changes in appetite, sleep patterns

- Irritability, anger, worry, agitation, anxiety

- Pessimism, indifference

- Loss of energy, persistent tiredness

- Feelings of guilt, worthlessness

- Inability to concentrate, indecisiveness

- Inability to take pleasure in former interests, social withdrawal

- Unexplained aches and pains

- Recurring thoughts of death and suicide

Depression can be caused by several factors or a combination of them, including but not limited to genetic factors, imbalance in certain brain chemicals, difficult life events, hormonal changes in women, certain thinking patterns, presence of certain other diseases, and medication side effects.

About half of those people experiencing one depression will have the disorder again, and 50 percent of all depression patients experience a depressive episode between ages twenty and fifty. The average age of onset is about forty, although many people experience their first episode in their late teens or early adulthood (fifteen to thirty) or even younger. Depression affects women twice as often as men.[4]

Among all medical illnesses, depression is the leading cause of disability in the United States and many other developed countries, and it costs the U.S. economy $70 billion annually in medical expenditures, lost productivity, and other expenses.[5]

Depression often occurs along with other illnesses, including cancer, heart disease, diabetes, eating disorders, and substance abuse disorders.[6] It causes a greater decrease in general health than any of the chronic diseases—angina, arthritis, asthma, and diabetes. Depression is the cause of more than two-thirds of the thirty-two thousand reported suicides in the United States each year.[7]

Depression is treatable. Up to 80 percent of those treated for depression show some degree of improvement in their symptoms, generally within four to six weeks of beginning medication, psychotherapy, or a combination of these treatments. Medication and psychotherapy are about equally effective for treating depression; receiving both may be the most effective treatment.[8]

Even for people with chronic major depression or bipolar disorder, *recovery*—the reclaiming of a meaningful, productive life—is possible. Recovery occurs through a variety of approaches, including medicine and other medical treatments, psychotherapy, support groups, family and friends' support, assistance with job placement, and creative therapies such as writing.

# *Describing Depression*

One of the most brilliant personal memoirs of depression was penned by Pulitzer prize–winning author William Styron in his book *Darkness Visible: A Memoir of Madness* (Random House, 1990). In considering his experience, Styron pointed out, with some irritation, that in our language and society we lack a proper word for the illness of depression: the word "depression" is, he writes, "used indifferently to describe an economic decline or a rut in the ground, a true wimp of a word for such a major illness. . . . [F]or over seventy-five years the word has slithered innocuously through the language like a slug, leaving little trace of its intrinsic malevolence and preventing, by its very insipidity, a general awareness of the horrible intensity of the disease when out of control."[9]

Members of a support group for mood disorders in Palo Alto, California, recently gave these descriptions of what their depression would look like if they could visualize it: a tornado, a dark cloud, a fall off a cliff, a many-headed monster, a cracked mirror. Diverse as these images are, they all dramatically convey a sense of fright and despair. In addition, all agreed that if you haven't "been there," you can't truly imagine how a severe depression feels.

My own depression often appears to me as a dark fog that has enshrouded my head and body. It may appear as I chew my morning granola or drive down the highway or sit listening in a meeting. Suddenly I notice my limbs are heavy, and I want to escape into sleep. I have been punctured, and all the spark, curiosity, and volition have drained from me, leaving me uncaring about the world around me. Fear rises in me as I watch sadness tighten my throat and sense the heaviness of a leaden ball in my chest. Though I try to control it, deep sadness quickly pervades every part of my being, like strong tree roots that cannot be stopped even by concrete. Stunned, though I've experienced this onslaught many, many times before, an image arises in my mind's eye, like in a dream: I am standing in a long black dress at a funeral for everyone I love. It seems to me that this imagined anguish matches what I feel. And in that hopeless moment, I'm certain that, as there is no chance of these beloved people's return, there is no hope of this despair ever lifting.

## The Stigma Surrounding Depression

One of the unique characteristics of depression is the stigma that it still carries. Depression is an illness that affects not just one person at a time, but can alter relationships the sufferer has with others as well. If you've felt uncomfortable with your symptoms around your friends, coworkers, even your doctor, you may have experienced the stigma that often surrounds both situational depression and medical depression.

Stigma has been defined as "a mark of shame or discredit."[10] Stigma and depression are inseparable in our society, despite all the facts that science and medicine have unearthed in recent years about how depression is truly a biologically based brain disorder—not a personal weakness. If you had a kidney disorder or heart disease, no one would tell you to "Pull yourself together" or "Get over it," yet many of us have heard such comments about our illness. Although it shouldn't be treated differently, we often still feel ashamed when telling others that we're suffering from depression.

This is important because nearly two-thirds of Americans with a diagnosable mental disorder do not seek treatment, and much of this is due to the stigma or discrimination they expect to feel.[11] One of the most unkind aspects of stigma is that it can invade our own thoughts and feelings, becoming internalized. Have you ever told yourself, "I shouldn't be depressed"? This sort of self-criticism is common. It can lead to feeling defeated by the illness, which can exacerbate symptoms and even lead people to discontinue treatment.

Putting our pain—about depression or stigma—into words can be very healing for several reasons. It helps us identify our feelings and separate ourselves from them. And, as you'll learn, writing allows us to create stories about our lives and to find different perspectives, both of which are very healing. In addition, writing about self-stigmatization can be a crucial way of identifying what's happening inside, what judgments and expectations we carry, and in what ways we might respond to these inner decrees. It can help us sift out these aspects of our depression and examine them so that we can make conscious decisions about what we tell ourselves and what actions we want to take.

*to write*

### THE STIGMA OF DEPRESSION

Have you felt stigmatized about your depression? Has anyone treated you inappropriately upon seeing your changed behavior or when you told of your depression? Write about any times you've felt discriminated against because of your illness and how it felt.

### YOUR DEPRESSION'S CHARACTER

How does your depression look to you? How does it act and what does it say? Describe the images and scenes that come to you.

This piece, based on the prompt, "Give a voice to your mental health condition," describes the character of the writer's illness and her feelings about it.

### ANOTHER VOICE

*The Beast* by Kate V.

This exercise conjures up monsters in closets with matted fur and fangs and misunderstood eyes. If my bipolar were a monster, I think I would want to try to love it. I cannot allow it to be too repulsive or angry right now because I feel weak. No, I don't think I could survive a hostile or volatile beast. So I will make it whimper, and feel pain, too. My disorder is like a big beast that cannot help itself, that frightens and disrupts and then suffers for it; like the creature in *Beauty and the Beast*. The beast is under a magical curse and he is gentle hearted and misled and dying. I envision myself as the house he resides in, overgrown with vines and brambles and haunted by his living presence. I don't remember what the beast says in the animated Disney movie or the fairytale theater video I grew up with or the nearly silent black-and-white masterpiece I studied in a college course on the philosophy of film. I don't think the beast needed to speak, there was so much visible. I wish my disorder were a beast like Belle's, a beast I could love.

# This Writing Is Therapeutic, But Not "Therapy"

After her first visit, a new member of my writing group recently exclaimed, "This is the best therapy I've ever had!" This assessment is frequently made by these writers with depression, most of whom have participated in psychotherapy, sometimes for years. When something allows them to feel better emotionally, particularly if it also involves some psychological self-examination, they, quite reasonably, consider it "therapy."

This issue can be tricky for semantic reasons. Broadly, a therapy is something that makes you feel better; it heals or rehabilitates. One type of therapy, psychotherapy, is a frequently prescribed depression treatment. It may be used with either individuals or groups. Psychotherapy is conducted by licensed practitioners and comprises a broad range of approaches but utilizes specific psychological techniques to uncover and affect a client's thoughts, emotions, and behaviors. Psychotherapy and writing do have some effects in common: both explore emotions; both aim for self-reflection, insight, and understanding; both can improve psychological and physical health.

*Literature contains elements of therapy; therapy contains elements of literature.*

—Nicholas Mazza, *Poetry Therapy: Theory and Practice*

Despite these similarities, the work done in our writing group for depression is not group psychotherapy. Pat Schneider, founder of Amherst Writers and Artists, who developed writing workshops for low-income women, then expanded them for a wide variety of populations, describes her work in her book *Writing Alone and with Others* (Oxford University

Press, 2003): ". . . *[T]he writing workshop is not group therapy.* In a good writing workshop, this healing occurs individually, often secretly, and in utmost privacy. There is no pressure on the participant to read what has been written. The leader of the workshop may never know the effect of the writing workshop on the lives of its members."[12]

My writing group operates along similar lines—while it may be therapeutic in the sense that it helps with emotional healing, it is *not* a form of psychotherapy, including group therapy.

## Writing Is Art

Art can be defined as the product of self-expression based on your exploration of self and the world. But art also arises from carefully developed skills. Most of the writing techniques in this book and in the groups I lead for people with depression are for spontaneous writing, unlike in a critique group where writers hone their craft with many revisions. Still, writing to ease depression empowers each person to speak out and express her experiences and her interpretation of the world; this is creating art. As Pat Schneider describes it, "The purpose [of the writing workshops] is to free the voice of the writer. . . . What we offer is respect for the workshop participant *as an artist*."[13]

Whether you are seeking a new, creative adjunct therapy for your depression or have written on your health for years and now want to discover new techniques, the primary goals of writing to ease depression are these: the exploration of yourself and your relationship to your world, and expressing what you find. Writing offers us the opportunity to reflect and to synthesize a product—to create art as we speak our own, unique truth. My main role, as a writer and as a peer who has "been there," is to encourage you, a person with depression, to find, probe, and develop the subjects and writing techniques that are most conducive to healing for you personally, to allow you to be the artist that you already are.

# Writing Helps Moods in Many Contexts

Numerous well-known authors and poets throughout history have used writing to cope with depression, including conditions we would now diagnose as major depression or bipolar disorder. There are copious reports and self-reports from others of the benefits of journaling and other writing techniques for managing emotions. And writers coping with depression in the group at Stanford have described how writing improves their moods in many ways: Writing helps to "build self-esteem," "make sense of my anger and confusion," "challenge my existing interpretation of my life," "validate my experience," "give emotional release," and "clear my mind and spirit."

Writing can help heal people's thoughts and feelings but also their physical health and spiritual life, as we'll discuss in coming chapters. Writing has been used to promote psychological healing in widely diverse populations who have suffered traumas or are deemed "at risk" for future life difficulties, including:

- HIV/AIDS patients

- Breast cancer patients

- Holocaust survivors

- Inner-city children and teens

- Abused women and children

- Prison inmates

- Veterans of the Iraq, Afghanistan, and Vietnam wars

- Adult children of alcoholics

- Elderly nursing home residents

- Homeless people

- Professional caregivers: physicians, nurses, chaplains

You may already know of one particularly inspirational project in which a new teacher helped "unteachable, at-risk" high schoolers in a very violent neighborhood to journal about their lives. Their work resulted in a book, *The Freedom Writers Diary* (Broadway Books, 1999), and the recent movie *Freedom Writers*. The process allowed these adolescents to transform themselves into authors, community activists, and college-bound students. It's clear that writing can help dramatically in many people's growth and healing.

## A Therapeutic Approach to Writing

Research studies and anecdotal evidence both show that certain methods of writing are most healing. In my writing group, we have found that incorporating several types of exercises, in specific order, in our meetings provides the greatest therapeutic benefit. Even if you're writing independently, you may want to consider how you can apply this approach to your own writing practice. I usually include three steps in my classes:

1. A **warm-up exercise** helps everyone become mentally present in the room and ease into focusing on writing. This exercise is based on a concrete, simple, often one-word prompt from which you can write very literally or, if desired, go into a more emotional realm (for example, the ocean, your childhood bedroom, purple, your first car). Ten minutes is usually a good amount of time for a warm-up.

2. Next, we move into deeper feelings with an **exploration exercise**. This is usually a more serious prompt dealing with emotions or past experiences that might be somewhat challenging and which in some cases deals directly with the writer's depression (for example, describe one of your parents and your relationship. What depression symptoms are you dealing with today? How did you feel when you were first diagnosed with depression? How have your religious or spiritual beliefs changed

since you were a child?). This exercise generally requires more time than the first one, perhaps twenty minutes. I also frequently offer an alternative exploration exercise suggestion for use by anyone who feels too uncomfortable with the main topic on that day.

3. We then generally do a **reflection exercise**. While still thought provoking, this prompt is useful in bringing writers' mood and focus back from the exploration writing. It allows people to balance more enjoyable feelings with the challenging ones and to finish the two-hour class period on a positive note. This exercise usually takes ten to twenty minutes, depending on the time available (for example, describe a mentor you've had and how she or he helped you; tell the story of a mysterious thing that happened to you; describe where you think evolution is taking humans; describe a place that feels very safe for you).

What if you're writing on your own to ease depression? You don't need to follow this class structure, although you could if you were writing for forty-five to sixty minutes at one sitting. Instead, be aware of the different types of topics you might undertake on a particular day and do what feels most healing to you at the time. In this book's exercises, I suggest topics plucked from all of these categories, not necessarily in order. I encourage you to explore a variety of these prompts. Challenge yourself, but don't overwhelm yourself. If one thing doesn't appeal to you, move on to another. This is for *you*.

*to write*

### DREAM IMAGES

**Many forms of art, including writing, have been inspired by dreams. Think of a vivid dream you've had and describe its images, sounds, and textures in as much detail as possible.**

Here's what one member of our group, a writer and a painter, wrote after reflecting about dreams.

**ANOTHER VOICE**

## *Dreams* by Robert Voss

I dream of colors, forms, and shapes. I dream of the sensual urge that informs how I approach the canvas. The colors swing and sway in contrast, sexual shapes hinting at the love within. The shapes morph like a paddle through water. The shapes change to take on mathematical quanta, physical realities bound to an equation speaking of emotional turbulence. For after all there is little difference between art and science. All shapes and colors that hit the canvas have a foundation in math, a connection to physics. . . . And in the end I wish I could paint my dreams, for these alone seem to be beyond this corporeal world.

# Chapter 3

# Science Says Writing Helps Your Health

*As the number of studies increased, it became clear that writing was a far more powerful tool for healing than anyone had ever imagined.*

—James W. Pennebaker, *Writing to Heal*

As I've described, writing helped me climb out of severe depression, and students in my writing groups report tremendous improvements. But can any of writing's effects be measured? Indeed they can, says the scientific world, which has exploded in recent years with data about specifically *what* kinds of writing benefit health and *how* the process affects body and mind. This chapter describes how researchers are shedding light on the mysteries of the writing-health connection and how you can make the most of their findings.

## Traumas and Secrets

Psychological researchers have long known that traumas or significant emotional crises are stressful to the mind and body. This effect is so dramatic that traumatized people have higher rates of depression and other ailments and are even more likely to die of cancer and heart disease than the general population. What is it about these traumas that leads to such health problems? In the 1980s, researcher James W. Pennebaker (now at the University of Texas at Austin) and his team found a clue. They studied people who had experienced a life-changing trauma in childhood such as the death of a family member, the divorce of parents, physical abuse, or a sexual trauma. They discovered that people who had such an experience but *kept it secret* were at much higher risk for both major and minor illnesses than those who spoke about it. Their different levels of health were easy to discern: the secret-keepers went to the doctor 40 percent more often.[1]

Other scientists soon expanded on these findings and found, for example, that people whose spouses had committed suicide or died suddenly in accidents had better health in the following year if they discussed that trauma.[2] In other research, gays and lesbians who were out of the closet had fewer health problems than those who did not disclose their sexual orientation.[3] After numerous studies, the conclusion became clear: not discussing your important life issues puts your health at significantly greater risk.

These results led to the experiment that would launch this field of writing and health. Psychologists asked the following: if keeping major secrets is bad for health, can talking—or writing—about them *improve* your health? To answer this, Pennebaker recruited average college freshmen to write in his lab for fifteen minutes a day for four consecutive days. Half of them were assigned by the flip of a coin to write about traumatic issues in their lives (what researchers call *expressive writing*); the others were told to write on superficial topics. Over their first four studies, they found that the students who wrote on personal traumas, who often were moved to tears during their writing sessions, felt the need to visit the doctor for illnesses at just half the usual rate in the following months—their health actually got better.[4] This result and the dozens that corroborated it were so strong that they surprised even the scientists, as they showed that writing is an amazingly powerful tool for healing.

## Writing Helps Your Mood, Body, and Behavior

We've seen that expressive writing led to fewer doctor visits. But why— what does writing do to us? Many things, it turns out. In *Writing to Heal* (New Harbinger Publications, 2004), Pennebaker groups the changes documented in dozens of studies into psychological effects, biological effects, and behavioral effects, as summarized below.

First, this type of writing leads to mood changes. Immediately after writing about a trauma, many people report feeling sadder for an hour or so. But this soon gives way to greater happiness and less negativity as well as a sense of increased insight in the next weeks or months. In particular, there are fewer reports of general anxiety, rumination, and *depressive symptoms* after writing.[5]

Second, many labs have found this kind of writing has other immediate biological effects. Drops in blood pressure and heart rate, changes in brainwave patterns, increases in general immune system function, and altered skin conduction (like that measured in lie-detector tests) have all been observed after writing about a trauma. For people with chronic health problems, writing can help in a variety of ways for many months: asthmatics develop better lung function; rheumatoid arthritis sufferers have decreased pain; AIDS patients have increased white blood cell counts. Writing significantly changes your biology.[6]

Finally, writing changes the way you act. In terms of social life, people tend to talk more, listen better, feel more socially comfortable, and be better friends in the weeks following their expressive writing experience. In other studies, it helped alleviate anger and rumination in laid-off high-tech workers—and even led them to interact with others differently, leading to more success in their interviews for new jobs. Writing also aids performance in some situations. For example, college students earn higher grades after a writing study. This is thought to be due to an increase in what psychologists call "working memory," which is the portion of the brain's memory available to accomplish many types of cognitive tasks and to problem solve.[7]

So what do all of these amazing changes mean? As researchers Stephen J. Lepore and Joshua M. Smyth put it, "It is clear that expressive writing modulates activity in emotional, cognitive, and physiological systems, although the precise manner in which it does so, the clinical significance of these various changes, and who is affected in this way have yet to be fully determined."[8] In other words—we know writing changes us, but we're still learning *how* it works, *what* this means medically, and *who* exactly is changed by it. The changes triggered by these expressive writing experiments are very real—but it will take a lot more research to learn all the details.

Edward J. Murray, a psychologist at the University of Miami, not involved in Pennebaker's original studies, questioned these findings at first but eventually concluded that "writing seems to produce as much therapeutic benefit as sessions with a psychotherapist."[9] For now, we can definitely conclude that holding in thoughts and feelings, such as secrets and reactions to trauma, builds up physical and emotional stress. These stresses can then increase many types of health risks and illness symptoms. And now it's clear that writing about these difficult experiences can allow us to change psychologically and physically. In addition, it can help us *organize* our thoughts and feelings and develop more *insight*—in fact, in the months after writing about a trauma, most people report having a better understanding of the event and of themselves.[10]

## Guidelines for Writing about Trauma

Certain methods of writing about your traumatic life events are more effective than others in improving health. How can you take advantage of them? Pennebaker has developed some writing suggestions based on the research results of many scientists. These are summarized below from Pennebaker's descriptions in his books *Opening Up* (Avon, 1990)[11] and *Writing to Heal* (New Harbinger Publications, 2004).[12]

- To begin, set aside *twenty minutes* when you won't be interrupted.

- Start by writing about an *emotional turmoil* that is bothering you right now—the one you keep dreaming about or lying awake thinking about. (Digging up issues that you've already dealt with isn't particularly helpful.) Then, writing continuously, follow where your writing about this event takes you. If you reach a point where you don't know what to write, just repeat what you've already written.

- Writing about *older traumas* seems to be somewhat more useful than writing about very recent ones. In studies of Holocaust survivors, even the expression of decades-old unprocessed traumas was very beneficial. In contrast, a trauma that occurred just a couple of weeks ago is likely to be so fresh that you can't yet organize it. Also, write only about traumas or crises you are consciously aware of. Despite interest in repressed memories, assume for this purpose that if you don't remember it, it didn't occur.

- *Self-reflection* is key in this type of writing. To enhance self-reflection, the following techniques are most beneficial: acknowledge your emotions openly; try to construct a coherent, meaningful story about the trauma; and, if you can, even try switching perspectives from your own to those of others as you write. In addition, research indicates that writing about both thoughts and feelings surrounding the event is much more effective than writing about just one or the other.

- In *constructing a story*, you typically will need to include the same things you include when telling a story to a friend: the setting, the characters involved, what happened, the consequences of that event, and the value or meaning you assign to it.

- Some psychologists believe that writing is most helpful when it involves particularly unwanted, unexpected traumas. However, there's no indication that writing about lesser turmoil is harmful. Other data show that writing on strongly positive emotions is beneficial, too. For example, the obsessive feelings of love can be akin to trauma—we seek to understand them, too. In writing on any emotional upheaval, acknowledge the negative feelings and keep an eye out for the positive ones—having a *balance of negative and positive* words in a piece of writing is most beneficial.

- Other kinds of words people use in their writing have been shown to affect the benefits they receive, too. Stories are most effective when they show connections between events by including a lot of *causal words* (for example, "cause," "effect," "because," "reason," "rationale") and when they demonstrate understanding by using a lot of *insight words* (for example, "realize," "know," "meaning").

- Having some *reflection time* after writing is thought to be a good idea in order to help any sadness dissipate and to consolidate your thoughts.

- Finally, researchers agree with what my group has found: it's fine to use *either a pen or a computer* for this type of writing.

## Writing Is Not a Panacea

The data that's been accumulated on writing and healing is impressive and intriguing. But while writing may help many diverse *symptoms*, it's unlikely to *cure* ailments—including depression—on its own, and there are even very rare times when it may make things worse (see chapter 5 on writing with psychosis or dissociation). You should be aware of a few caveats.

Studies have not directly examined how a population of people diagnosed with depression has responded to writing. Rather, the depressive symptoms shown by a general population have been measured, and they have improved. It's also important to realize that the data doesn't answer such broad questions as whether writing about your emotions can help you "deal with" your life.

Not all writing experiences help everyone. All the results described here are of course averages from relatively large groups of people, and individuals respond uniquely. Still, it's encouraging that it has been shown that writing's beneficial effects do not vary with culture, language, education level, or writing ability.

## *The Data Is Encouraging*

Whether or not you are a scientist, you as a writer should appreciate that there is hard evidence—psychological, biological, and behavioral—that writing can have myriad health benefits. While most of the research so far has focused specifically on writing about traumatic experiences and writing for particular lengths of time over specific numbers of days, it seems reasonable to think that some of these results may carry over to other types of writing as well. Further research will tell. For now, as you begin writing to ease your depression, bear in mind that, happily, these experiments prove that, in at least some cases, writing can change you.

### *to write*

### AN EXPERIMENT IN HEALING

In many, many research studies on different groups of people, the basic structure of writing about a difficult event for twenty minutes a day for four days in a row has been shown to be effective. Although you're still toward the beginning of this book, now is your first chance to try this experiment for yourself if you feel comfortable doing so. I've tried this myself numerous times and have felt much more "together" afterward. Think of an upheaval, a trauma, or a disturbing event in your past; it may be directly linked to your depression or it may not be. Then follow the bulleted points given earlier in this chapter to write about it. In *Writing to Heal*, Pennebaker suggests that after you write on each of the four consecutive days, take a moment to note the following on a scale of 0 to 10—to what degree you expressed your deepest thoughts and feelings; to what degree you currently feel sad or upset; to what degree you currently feel happy; and how valuable and meaningful today's writing was for you.[13]

Now you may want to conduct your own experiment and see whether you find this particular, scientifically described form of writing helpful to you as you strive to ease your depression.

# Chapter 4

# *What about All Those Depressed Authors?*

*Those who have become eminent in philosophy, politics, poetry, and the arts have all had tendencies toward melancholia.*

—Aristotle

Dim memories of high school English class may be cropping up for you now—reading *Hamlet* and *The Bell Jar* or discussing the lives and deaths of Hemingway and Woolf. Whether your teacher pointed it out or you made the connection on your own, you probably saw the frequent association between writers and depression. If depression is so common among writers, you may be wondering why this book is encouraging you to write to ease your own depression. It turns out that depression's connection to writing, and to the arts in general, is complex.

It's true that over the eons that humans have been writing, some have been describing the melancholy they experience. But writers have also used writing itself to lift mood; the history is abundant. "Writing has long been held forth as a treatment for depression,"[1] says psychiatrist and author Peter Kramer in *Against Depression* (Viking, 2005). He cites Renaissance authors such as Michel de Montaigne and Robert Burton. Burton explained, "I write of melancholy, by being busy to avoid melancholy."[2] In modern times, some authors, such as Isabelle Allende, report they have written themselves *out* of depressions;[3] others report writing to simply survive. Numerous contemporary authors, including novelist Graham Greene, have even described their use of writing to manage depressions that were so bad they were considering suicide. As Greene wrote, "Sometimes I wonder how all those who do not write, compose or paint can manage to escape the madness, the melancholia, the panic fear which is inherent in the human situation."[4]

At the very least, it's important for you as a writer to take heart from the many examples of authors and poets who have written so brilliantly, and to healing effect, during dire periods of their lives. But is this connection between writing and depression all based on a few fascinating characters like these, or is there truly a greater association between writing, or other arts, and depression or other mental illness? And if this idea is borne out, *why* is there this creative connection—and what does it mean for those who want to find relief from their own depression?

## Writers and Depression: The Connection Is Real

Don't be confused by the idealistic notion sometimes fostered in our society that writers and artists are always "mad." For example, the suffering genius behind the artist Vincent van Gogh's twirling stars and crinkled irises has been dissected and popularized in song, theater, film, and books. And unfortunately such recasting has often led to a sense of romance rather than horror around his ultimately fatal mental illness. Museum goers and art historians have pondered whether van Gogh's artistic brilliance derived from his disorder or flourished despite it. Is "great wit" really "to madness near allied,"[5] as commonly described, or is this perception unrealistic fluff?

At long last, in recent years, solid studies of this relationship have revealed that not only is the writing-depression association real, but it is stronger than many expected. However, it is not as simple to tease apart as you might think.

One of the most carefully controlled studies of writers and mood disorders such as depression was conducted by Nancy C. Andreasen, a professor of psychiatry at the University of Iowa, which is also the home of the prestigious Iowa Writer's Workshop. Andreasen took advantage—over the course of many years—of this nearby pool of eminent writers and studied the frequency and types of psychiatric illnesses in thirty of them. Their interviews and psychological test results were compared with thirty equally educated, age-matched comparison subjects whose work did not require high levels of creativity.

Andreasen's results were dramatic, as she recounts in her book *The Creating Brain* (Dana Press, 2005).[6] As these writers described their histories, she found that not just some, but the majority of them met the criteria for either depression or bipolar disorder. Most of them had, in fact, been treated for their illness, whether through medication, psychotherapy, or hospitalization. *The writers were more than twice as likely as the nonwriters to have depression* and more than four times as likely to have some form of bipolar disorder. Taken together, 30 percent of the controls displayed some type of mood disorder, compared to an enormous 80 percent of the writers. The rate of alcoholism, which frequently co-occurs with depression, was also more than tripled in the writer group.

Andreasen's results confirm the long-standing notion that depression is linked to creativity, but it's important to note that this connection is much weaker than that between bipolar disorder and creativity. Also, the numbers of subjects in her studies were not very large, so the strength of these connections is hard to state precisely.

Other studies have confirmed the findings of the Writer's Workshop study. Kay Redfield Jamison, professor of psychiatry at Johns Hopkins University, collected information on the histories of mood disorders of forty-seven prominent British writers and visual artists, as she describes in *Touched with Fire* (The Free Press, 1993).[7] Although she did not study a control sample, she found that writers of various types did indeed have increased frequency of both depression and bipolar disorder. Playwrights showed the highest rate of having been *treated* for a mood disorder (62.5 percent), followed by poets (55.2 percent), novelists (25 percent), biographers (20 percent), and finally visual artists (12.5 percent), while the treatment rate in the general population was 5 percent.

These results are certainly impressive, but in interpreting Jamison's studies, it's important to keep in mind that depression and bipolar disorder, two different illnesses, both considered "mood disorders," can be difficult to separate when looked at in terms of treatment rates, not diagnostic criteria. Thus, while the link between creativity and bipolar disorder is strong, the link to depression itself is considerably weaker.

It's interesting to note that none of the writers in the Iowa Writer's Workshop study evidenced symptoms of schizophrenia. Although the relationship between creativity and schizophrenia is still unclear, Andreasen hypothesizes that the sustained concentration required of writers may be incompatible with this illness.[8] However, other creative fields, such as mathematics and physics, which rely upon sudden insights or following unusual hunches, may be able to coexist with this illness. Most of the evidence in this area is anecdotal. If you look retrospectively for not just schizophrenia but lesser schizotypal traits, such notables as Bertrand Russell, John Nash, Isaac Newton, and even Albert Einstein come up for consideration.

The question remains: are people with depression or other mental illnesses such as bipolar disorder really creatively inclined, or even creatively gifted? And if so, why? Let's take a closer look and see whether we can shed some light on your own creative tendencies.

## *Psychological Connections*

Several ideas have emerged around the issue of what exactly is the association between writing and depression. First, it's important to realize that Andreasen's writers consistently reported in their interviews that they were unable to be creative during a period of either depression or, if they experienced it, mania. Instead, they produced creative work *between* periods of illness, when their moods were relatively normal, since none of them experienced permanent or long-term abnormal moods.[9] However, Andreasen believes that some of these writers later actually drew upon some of the dramatic material gleaned from their periods of unusual moods and thoughts.

Thus, they use their healthy or *euthymic* periods to process, organize, and express the unconventional, even bizarre, experiences they had while depressed, resulting in very original ideas. The cause of the odd thoughts may be what scientists call *input dysfunction*, or a difficulty in filtering out all the sensory input we are all exposed to each day, a condition common in depression.[10]

An intriguing interpretation of the depression-creativity link reported in 2005 by Paul Verhaeghen and colleagues concludes that depression and creativity are in fact not directly related, but instead are both the result of another factor: the person's tendency to *ruminate*.[11] These scientists believe that this type of self-reflective musing, which focuses on inner thoughts, feelings, and memories, independently increases the risk of depression and triggers creative ability and behavior. The cause of depressives' extreme rumination may be decreased *cognitive inhibition*—related to input dysfunction, described above—which means the person must try to process an unusually broad range of sensory input. Thus, these researchers concluded the report of their findings: "So why do we sing the blues? . . . Both—the blues and the singing—appear to be rooted in a maybe all-too-closely examined life."[12]

## *The Value of Creativity versus Depression*

You may love the idea that your depression or bipolar disorder might mean you are special—bright, creative, productive, artistic. But would you be willing to surrender those traits if it meant you were never depressed again? It's a tough question for those who see some value in depression.

Psychiatrists as well as writers and other artists have long examined the question of what use depression might be to humans. Some have suggested that depression is actually beneficial to society because it results in creative advances that would otherwise not exist and may have even helped us evolve as a species. For example, author Edward Hoagland, writing in *Unholy Ghost: Writers on Depression* (Perennial, 2001), asserts: "People with sunny natures do seem to live longer than people who are nervous wrecks: yet mankind didn't evolve out of the animal kingdom by being unduly sunny-minded. Life was fearful and phantasmagoric, supernatural and preternatural. . . . [I]t was not just our optimism but our pessimistic premonitions . . . —our dread as well as our faith—that made us human beings."[13] Susanna Kaysen, author of the memoir of depression *Girl, Interrupted*, writing in *Unholy Ghost*, agrees: "I think melancholy is useful. In its aspect of pensive reflection or contemplation, it's the source of many books (even those complaining about it) and paintings, much scientific insight, the resolution of many fights between couples and friends, and the process known as becoming mature."[14]

This long-standing notion that depression is useful, especially to creativity, leads some contemporary artists and writers to question whether they want treatment, now that it is widely available. Psychiatrist Richard A. Friedman described a depressed professional photographer whom he treated with antidepressants.[15] She was initially reluctant to take the medicine for fear of its effect on her creative abilities. When she agreed, her photos did change dramatically from black and white to color, from dark urban pictures of the poor and homeless to happier street scenes of children playing and lovers arm in arm. As Friedman describes, she found this work "commercially successful but artistically mediocre"[16] and quit her medicine. However, after several months of deep depression, she reversed her decision and opted for happiness, regardless of its effect on her art.

Thus, though it may require such a trial or two, many writers and artists concerned with losing their edge do choose to be treated—though not without ambivalence. Also writing in *Unholy Ghost*, author and sociology professor David Karp concludes, "Through the years my attitude toward drugs has remained steady, a mixture of hostility and dependence."[17]

## Gaining Inspiration from Others

It is clear, from both anecdotes and science, that there is some association between writing and mood disorders. Of course, you don't need to experience a depression to be a writer or vice versa. Still, here you are, a person living with depression of some sort, beginning to write to help ease the pain. I think the most important conclusion to take from these tales of other creatives is that if they can do it, so can you, even when you're feeling depressed. In *Against Depression*, psychiatrist and author Peter Kramer concludes, "Depressives, it is said, have little energy, but that little they apply doggedly."[18] Keep writing as we look in the next chapters at more specific ways writing can help heal your depression.

*to write*

## WHY WRITE?

What is drawing you to write to ease your depression? Has writing given you aid before? Are you looking forward to particular effects it may have on you? Describe these feelings and hopes.

Here's a portion of an essay on what writing means to one group member.

**ANOTHER VOICE**

### *Writing* by Nancy Ruspil

Writing creates in me a safe place to be. I can float with the ocean waters or drudge through the swamps of life. Writing gives me the possibilities of saving myself from drowning or deciding to tread water as I explore the inner waterways of an experience. Writing allows me to quiet myself and be with my feelings. It is a place to be who and what I am.

Writing, like the wheels on a wheelchair, gives me the ability to get through life. It is essential to my emotional well being. I breathe and then I write. I do both to exist.

# Chapter 5

# *Writing for Your Mind, Heart, and Spirit*

*Creative work can act not only as a means of escape from pain,
but also as a way of structuring chaotic emotions and thoughts, numbing
pain through abstraction and the rigors of disciplined thought, and
creating a distance from the source of despair.*

—KAY REDFIELD JAMISON, *Touched with Fire*

Writing can help keep you whole. If you feel shattered or dented in your mind, your heart, or your spirit, it will help you reassemble and smooth yourself. This chapter examines how you can ease your depression by looking inside yourself at your thoughts and feelings and by looking out to the world around you at spiritual issues, too. We'll examine the way writing helps you discover and heal your thoughts and feelings first, because they are so intermingled, and then turn to how it can help you with your spirit. If you have been depressed—depressed where your heart feels dead and the world meaningless—writing can help you find signs of life again. This process won't remake you as you once were but rather will guide you to a more complete, more ordered, more authentic, more creative form. Writing will change you.

Writing will help you discover your *thoughts*. It will let you remember the wonderful and the terrifying things that have brought you to this moment. It will let you access and inventory where you are in life now that events, including depression, may have altered your relationships, your activities, and your self-image. And writing will help you regroup and envision the path you want to take as you move forward from here. Even when abstract thoughts are hard to hold in your mind, you can reflect and conjure and plan on paper, one word at a time.

Writing will help you discover your *feelings,* too. By describing yourself and your current state, you are granted entry into your authentic emotions—beyond the superficial "depressed" label that you may have learned to use for yourself. And writing about those feelings can help you deeply experience them, even the ones that have been lying dead beneath the flatness of depression. It can help you acknowledge the hell you may have gone through, validate how it may still pain you, and digest those feelings to bring you into a new place and perspective. And writing will let you notice and cultivate new feelings too, be they calmness, hope, satisfaction—or even pride at filling a page or two with words on a tough day.

> *[Through writing] I think more logically and completely. [It provides] continuity in an ever-changing outside world.*
>
> —BEN

Thoughts and feelings are, of course, inexorably entwined. Discussing them separately here is only done to point out that the breadth and the depth of the writing process can affect you in myriad ways when you write on different days and topics, at different points in your depression, even from one sentence to the next. As you gain writing experience, you may discover that both your thoughts and your feelings change every time you put pen to paper.

## *Help for Your Thoughts*

Let's consider just how writing can alter the way we think about simple or even complex issues. Here are some specific ways writing can develop and stimulate your thoughts.

Writing offers a **context** within which to view your life. When you write about a holiday memory of decorating a Christmas tree as a young boy along with six rowdy big brothers, you immediately find yourself connecting to who you were and what role you played in the group as well as to the season and the year when this occurred. In general, the process of writing grounds your thoughts and reveals the places you occupy within your family, work, and community, and within your life history and the greater world.

Writing can also lead to **clarity** of thought. It sometimes triggers insights and your recollection of memories in a way that nothing else does. You might write in your journal about your difficult boss and discover that he frustrates you most when he judges you in the tone of voice your father used to take when report cards came out. The word-by-word nature of writing means you must make events linear to record them. Thus, you'll often get a clearer picture of what happened, how, and why.

Shaping your view of events into story form offers **organization** of your disparate thoughts and lets you uncover new perspectives of your own or appreciate those of other people. Writing the tale of an auto accident you were in, for example, forces you to describe details in the exact order in which they occurred. Then, as you look at the picture of the whole situation, you might realize that you really weren't at fault at all, despite the other driver blaming you.

Writing can help you create a **plan**. It can provide both a record of your thoughts and a bold, concrete method for determining what to do next, in terms of your relationships, activities, treatment, and recovery from depression. If you want to go back to work after a depressed period, you can make lists of your goals and their subgoals and the baby steps you can take to reach each one. You can consider who you'll need to ask for help and you can develop a time line and an action plan.

It is often easier to **share** your thoughts after writing about them. If you are anxious about telling your new doctor about a difficult past breakup, you may want to write first about that troubled time in order to pick out the key points you want to make. By making your ideas visible and more ordered, your writing may enable you to more comfortably communicate ideas to those around you, including your loved ones, doctors, or peers, if you so choose.

# *Awakening New Thoughts*

I was horrified when I gained eighty pounds within a few months while taking one antipsychotic medicine I tried after all of the others had failed me. This new drug eliminated the disturbing voices I was hearing and odd visions I was seeing, but this side effect felt awful. I was only able to reverse the weight gain later when I discontinued that medicine as a new one became available. I still wince as I think of having to face old friends at a party on a visit to my hometown soon after expanding several clothing sizes, despite my struggles to diet and exercise. I wrote recently on the painful anticipation of weakening friendships and judgmental attitudes I felt at that time.

> Though I knew my supportive husband and mother would be there, I feared I'd feel lost and alone. What would these people think of me? I imagined horrible judgments being passed on me by people who hadn't seen me for years—since I wore my white satin wedding gown, tailored to a slim waist. They had all heard that I had mental health problems; now they'd think I had lost control of my body too—and that both were my fault, just a lack of willpower.
>
> "If she really wanted to, she could pull herself together and go back to work and lose some weight," I imagined them whispering to each other. "She showed so much promise when she was younger; it's too bad she's let herself go." Even if they kept their words polite, I dreaded silent condemnations from their looks of surprise and pity. People who had once loved me would turn away, not knowing how to talk with a mentally ill person. I realized that they all had probably conversed with heavy people before, but not to a person whose life had become largely defined by mood swings. I craved support from them but expected to feel their disapproval.

In that writing I reflected on how my sadness and fear of rejection by people I cared about hurt terribly. But I was also surprised to discover an angle that hadn't occurred to me before: my body-image concerns, while not insignificant, reflected my greater concerns at the time that these people, who had heard of my chronic mental illness, would treat me differently because of that disability. I feared their reaction to my depression more than their reactions to my body.

By writing out my fears, I *organized* my thoughts and found more *clarity* than I had gotten from just ruminating about the situation. Then I drew a conclusion near the end when I wrote, "I realized. . . ." This led to finding *context* for where I was in the process of learning to deal with relationships in light of my mental health condition.

## to write

### AGING

**Writing can frequently change our thinking about even a very difficult issue when we record our observations in addition to our feelings, then reflect and try to draw a conclusion. Describe your own observations about aging—your own or the aging of a friend or relative. After you've written for about ten minutes, see what conclusions you can draw—but don't stop; discover them in the course of your continuous writing.**

In the following piece, a group member gathered her thoughts and observations and reflected on her parents' aging process.

### ANOTHER VOICE

### *Aging* by Meryl

My mother turned eighty-nine this past Saturday. But I need to come to terms with the fact that she is aging. Not just physically, but in her mind. The neurologist has prescribed meds for her so she won't forget so much—forget if she took her various pills at 8 A.M., forget the people she met last week, forget how to make a phone call or use the phone book, forget what she read in a book today. Is there really a pill that can slow down the aging process and call a halt to the inevitable decline of memory? Surely it is the size of a horse pill and powerful too. But what's truly remarkable is that my mother can remember word for word poems she learned in elementary school, and songs too. She can sing songs from so many different times of her life. I wonder where the brain logs in the words and melody of a song. At least, in my mother's case, songs are there to stay . . . in her head and in her heart.

On the other hand, my father at ninety-two remembers names, dates, places, and historical details galore. He has a memory of remarkable proportions. He could *be* a walking history book. I wonder how my parents' daily life goes by with him remembering everything and she remembering very little. They must love and understand each other so deeply to be able to manage and live through this kind of major change in their long, long lives.

## *Help for Your Feelings*

If you've ever written in a journal, you have probably discovered that feelings can surface surprisingly quickly and strongly. You may also have found that these emotions change midstream at times, or that your feelings change after you put down the pen. Let's look at some specific ways writing can unearth and validate your emotions.

Writing is a means of **revealing** your emotions about the past and the present, both positive and negative. Consider what happens when you run into an old friend after years. If you feel conflicting emotions, or just feel confused, write about it—you may discover that you never forgave her for her high school prank but that you also feel sorry for her now.

The process of writing can allow you to **recognize** and face the reality of events and situations and their effects on you, in a time and manner that works for you. I've seen members of my group write and emotionally "discover" that they had been hurt badly, even abused, by someone in the past. Even if they previously knew the facts, sometimes writing in a safe place brings the associated emotions to the surface.

For many people, it is writing's cathartic effects, or **release**, that are most powerful. It can be a safe means of letting out anger, grief, and other difficult emotions, in particular. Allowing yourself to write freely about some annoyance at your partner that you've been holding in may release powerful emotions that you only suspected were there. After writing about how really angry you are, you could even write further to decide how you want to act on these newfound emotions.

Your words can also lead you to a **resolution** of emotions. As your writing enables you to better understand and accept events, ideas, and feelings, you may detect new emotions arising, including positive ones such as relief, comfort, joy, gratitude, pride at surviving, and courage to continue. We all probably know how a good cry can leave us feeling relief and perhaps even the bravery to go on despite a sad event; a good writing session can do the same.

Completing a piece of writing can result in **satisfaction** and a deep sense of accomplishment. On a depressed day, especially, you may savor the

*It is good to feel and name and express feelings.*

—Leslie

feeling that you have created something meaningful, expressive, and true to your authentic self when you complete even an honest ten minutes of journaling. There is a connection with yourself and the world that comes from expressing yourself through writing, as in any art.

## Discovering Feelings

The psychologists and nurses leading group therapy sessions on my first hospital stay consistently told me I had to start identifying my feelings as well as my thoughts. My reaction was to think to myself that I had just been through years of graduate training in how to think logically and rationally—who needs feelings? Still, I dutifully tried to determine my emotions. I was "frustrated" at my severe depression, I told the leaders repeatedly. They looked back at me patiently, as if waiting for me to go on. But I had nothing more to say. I wasn't being belligerent; that was just all I came up with on my internal inventory.

I wrote recently about how that list lengthened after I got home. Faced with the sudden lack of support and structure of the hospital environment,

I had picked up the notebook I'd been using to record doctor's visits and changes in medication dosages.

> I knew I was "frustrated" about my whole situation and I searched for an-other adjective. And as I slowly placed sentences on the page, my words and my emotions began to develop and evolve: would I always be this flat and hopeless and lethargic? Then it dawned on me: I must be afraid. Yes, I was very afraid of whatever might happen to me next. But I began to feel safer as I wrote to myself, knowing no one else would see these pages. Then I thought of my lifelong plans for an exciting, meaningful career imploding, leaving just a trail of smoke in my mind. This idea left me terribly sad, and I began to cry as I tried to describe that feeling. Then I asked myself: am I just not trying hard enough to get well? I reflected and was able to name another emotion: I was ashamed of my depression. There was something oddly liberating in actually identifying more pre-cisely how I felt badly, and then being brave enough to put it on paper— even paper I intended to hide or destroy. I noticed a new feeling too: an occasional twinge of pride as I chipped away at my emotions, which had become so frozen during this depression.

Gradually, through this writing process I identified emotions that I had forced underground so far that I didn't know they existed. Several feelings were *revealed* to me, and I was able to *recognize* and face them and some of the issues that connected to them. Even my halting early attempts to describe my emotions felt freeing once I got started, and that led to the beginning stages of *resolving* pain and cultivating more positive feelings.

## *to write*

### IDENTIFYING FEELINGS ON THE PAGE

**Think of a time when you felt ambivalent about a situation or even knew you were suppressing your feelings. An interaction with a friend or rela-**

tive we've not spoken with for a long time often leaves us in one of these states, for example. Or if you want to dig into a large life issue that you've only partially come to terms with, use that. Now write about the events of that situation and pay attention to the feelings that come up as you go; record those, too. Afterward, read what you wrote and see if you have identified any emotions that you were not previously aware of.

In this excerpt, Meryl used writing to identify and deeply explore her feelings around a very emotional time in her life.

**ANOTHER VOICE**

### *After Divorce* by Meryl

What I really want to say is that I want to love deeply again (after divorce), but I am afraid of being hurt, so I am confining myself to my home on weekends and trying to manage not getting depressed. I watch people falling in love on TV and start to cry. I walk the Baylands and see couples holding hands and start to cry. I go to a concert in the park and everyone there seems to be in a happy family or dancing as a couple and I start to cry. But it's really okay, all this crying, because I am tapping into the sadness that I have held in check in order to march through the endless and agonizing details of divorce. My psychiatrist tells me that I got so angry to cover up my own deep feelings of hurt. When I strip away the anger, I feel the hurt, and it's big—bigger than I ever imagined it to be, [s]o big that once I found out at the end of May my divorce was finalized, I cried hours and hours and for all the days over the Memorial Day weekend.

It has to do with going down deep into my heart and letting my feelings of pain and hurt come out into the light. Wise old women who have gone through this before me say *now* is when the healing starts. Well if it is, it sure does hurt. But I will not run from the process. Bring it on. Come on and try to get me, you huge sadness. There is no way you are going to take me with you into a depression. You will not win. You did once and held me in your arms for five years but this time you will *not* be the victor. This time my True Self will emerge, whatever that is.

*to write*

**TELLING A FRIEND**

What would you like to tell a trusted person about your depression? Consider whether there are thoughts or feelings that you've never shared before, and write them to a nonjudgmental imaginary friend. Be sure to include your opinions and ideas (what you think) *and* your emotions and moods (what you feel) surrounding your symptoms and any related issues.

Afterward, reflect upon how this writing felt—did it offer any relief or comfort? Did it trigger any new ideas about your depression? Did it suggest anyone who you may want to confide in in the future?

## Help for Your Spirit, Too

"Describe your spiritual life."

I asked this of a writing group recently, and hands shot up.

"I'm not really religious," a student protested.

"I haven't gone to church for years," said another.

"Spirituality and religion are not the same things, and everyone has a spiritual life," I replied.

Whether you follow the tenets of a particular religion, have drifted or turned away from what you were raised with, have your own ideas about some higher power, or are a strict atheist, you have a spiritual life.

*I look for help in therapy, in relationships, and in faith in its broadest sense—the faith of the gardener, the faith of the lover, the faith of the writer.*

—JOSHUA WOLF SHENK, IN *Unholy Ghost*

Spirituality, I believe, refers to the way we understand the mysteries of the world around us and inside of us. How do you conceptualize love? Compassion? What happens when we die? Is there some higher power in the universe? How can we be happy? What about fate or coincidence? Where do we come from, and just what are we doing here? These are spiritual issues, ones we all must face in our lives and—if we are to dig deeply and search honestly—in our writing, too.

For those of us coping with depression, spiritual issues may feel especially urgent. And new questions may come up: Why did this happen to me? What does this mean about my role in the world? What can I do to relieve the pain? And can any good come from this experience? Writing can help you investigate and answer these questions and others for yourself.

## Benefits of Exploring Your Spirituality

Spiritual seekers over the ages have found myriad benefits to uncovering, defining, and fully embracing their beliefs. For many of us, a reassuring sense of clarity can arise from spiritual questioning and finding our own answers to eternal questions. Some, including those suffering from depression, have found relief and comfort from feeling that they are part of some larger plan in the universe; others may be reassured by the thought that events happen randomly and we cope as best we can.

*I honestly think in order to be a writer, you have to learn to be reverent. If not, why are you writing? Why are you here?*

—ANNE LAMOTT,
*Bird by Bird*

Sometimes a spiritual outlook provides a sense of meaning in your life, which can be especially important during times of despair. Indeed, I have known writing group members who come to feel that there is a reason, even a benefit, to their depressed experiences, be it to learn and grow as human beings, to develop compassion and understanding, or to assist others in their healing.

It turns out that spiritual seeking also carries health benefits. We can't directly measure the effects of something as ephemeral as spirituality. However, researchers have looked at how the body and mind's health correlates with two related issues: whether you describe yourself as a spiritual and/or religious person and whether you regularly take part in spiritual practices, such as attending religious services. The findings clearly demonstrate that each of these is both mentally and physically healthy. Study after study shows that people who consider themselves religious or spiritual, especially those who attend weekly religious services, tend to have fewer illnesses in general and to live significantly longer lives than those who don't.[1] This connection holds true for depression in particular, too. Dozens of studies have found, collectively, that religiously involved people have less depression, fewer depressive symptoms, and a greater likelihood of remission from depression.[2] Scientists theorize that attending religious services may be beneficial because they provide a strong network of personal support, which is known to be a health booster, and because they are correlated with the reduction of poor health habits such as smoking and drinking too much.

Practical application of such findings to treatment of depression is under study, too. For example, meditation, a component of many spiritual traditions, has been shown to be a useful adjunct to treatments for many health conditions, including depression. In addition, treatment of depressed religious people has been shown to be more effective when religious content is added to cognitive behavioral therapy or standard psychotherapy.

*to write*

## SPIRITUAL HELP

**Has exploring your spirituality ever helped you? Perhaps you discovered as a child that you felt safer or calmer after praying; maybe you've found that your mood eases when you meditate; you may have felt reassured in your beliefs by studying science. Describe that experience and then consider whether you still hold that helpful belief.**

Spiritual guidance is often important to those recovering from alcohol-related issues, not uncommon in the experience of people who have depression, as Rose describes on the next page.

### *Life Is Good* by Rose

Alcohol burns when I drink it. My husband was violent when he was drunk; he was violent sober too. Heavy memories weigh me down when I think of those frantic years—I am a survivor of a war zone.

This gives me another label: codependent. I go to meetings to learn about the disease, how it cascades along like a wild waterfall, wearing us down with loss, [leaving us] grieving our loved ones, our unattained dreams.

Yet, slowly light appears. I realize the alcoholic was suffering from a disease and is not evil. I learn to turn to God for my answers. Alcohol fades in God's love and light. I have choices today, and yes, life is good!

## *Applying Writing to Your Spiritual Exploration*

Writing enables some people to connect to their existing spiritual beliefs, which can be healing as they grapple with depression. For others, writing about spirituality during a time of depression may be more of an exploratory tool. Writing is an excellent way to capture your nascent spiritual ideas and understanding, and to recognize the wisdom that comes with them. You may find that writing on important questions allows you to reflect on your life's path and meaning and then to watch as your personal truths emerge from your words. In particular, life events related to your illness—from tragedies to times of wonder to pivotal moments of clarity—can often be identified and put into context by telling their stories on the page from a spiritual vantage point. I've also heard depressed group members share writing that demonstrates a universal truth—*I will find my way through this trial,* for example—that others can identify with and learn from, too.

> *To tell the story of the moments when we've suffered and then healed our essential wounds is to reveal a universal insight that extends far beyond the particulars.*
>
> —HAL ZINA BENNETT,
> *Write from the Heart*

"Mental illness can lead a person to seek a new spiritual path different from that of his or her family and friends,"[3] writes Catholic priest Jerome Stack, who has been a chaplain in psychiatric hospitals. Indeed, the crisis of depression left me wondering what spiritual viewpoints I really held in addition to my firm beliefs in scientific explanations of the universe. Writing turned out to be the thing that eased the way and let me discover ideas that I had paid little attention to before. Pondering the big issues of life on paper, bit by bit, was sometimes what kept me going when nothing else could move me.

When I was still reeling from one hospitalization for depression and trying to make sense of how and why this illness had hit me and what I was going to do about it, I was drawn to write about spiritual issues. And about this time, when I joined a Unitarian Universalist congregation—where all responsible religious and spiritual views are welcomed and respected—I was encouraged to conduct my own personal exploration.

As I continued writing nearly every day, month after month, I also found myself at bookstores perusing and buying books on spirituality. One thing I learned was that I had made writing a spiritual "practice" for myself. Spiritual practices, I learned, are activities that help many people strengthen their connections to the world around them and to their inner selves. Practices traditionally include prayer, meditation, following dietary rules, chanting, and other rituals, carried out either within or outside a defined religious setting. However, I also came to know people who consider dancing, weaving, or running to be their spiritual practice. For me, though, it was writing that allowed me to sift through and examine my inner life, to connect more strongly with what I found, and to gradually uncover information about how I conceived of the world, including how it had delivered me to such a depressed point. I recently recalled my thoughts of that period.

As a biologist, I accept the medical explanations that depression can be triggered by stressors—like my major life changes—and that my propensity for it is partially genetic. Clearly my brain's biochemistry is messed up somehow. But what else?

On one of the surveys the doctors had me take was a question asking, "Do you feel you are being punished?" What an odd question, I thought. I don't believe in a punitive God who might be disciplining me for some sin. But do I believe in God at all? I don't conceive of a God as a being watching me from somewhere. But since I was a kid, I've felt that people—and animals and other things—are connected somehow by a web or force or energy. I think that is my conception of God. I know other people have very different ideas, and I respect all of those very deeply too. Everyone's beliefs are valuable.

I also believe that people can cultivate positive traits, such as compassion, in themselves, as Buddhists suggest. Maybe even desiring to nurture such tendencies is due to some ephemeral positive force in the universe. I can't define it very well, but I believe I've felt it—and perhaps this too is my God—in the calm of meditations, in loving relationships, in the joy of being in nature. I think I've seen it in action too in coincidences and unusual events I've experienced at times.

I want to believe this exists. I want the comfort of feeling a part of something beneficent, something larger than myself. I want it in part because it gives me hope in the face of desperate depression. Is it enough to just want to believe in something that can't be seen or measured? This is a hard one for me. After much, much consideration, I've decided that this is okay for me in this case. No one can provide me "hard" evidence either way, and I think it is valid to choose to believe something if it serves me personally and it doesn't harm another in any way.

I came to realize that life stressors, including depression, provide tremendous opportunity for spiritual exploration, and writing about existential issues can prove fascinating, encouraging, and satisfying. Many of my group members have found that a writing practice can help not only with thoughts and emotions but also with a fuller comprehension of their own beliefs about their lives and their place in the immense scheme of what surrounds us.

*to write*

## THE BIG QUESTIONS

**What do you feel are the important "big questions" in life, and how do you respond to them? For example, you may feel that where we came from or what happens when we die are crucial issues for you to explore. Maybe you want to understand true love or the nature of depression. Start your writing by posing one or more big questions, and then describe your reactions to them.**

In this excerpt, a group member took on big issues and told of his beliefs about them.

**ANOTHER VOICE**

### *Big Questions* by Bill Scholtz

For me the big questions are "Who am I?" and "What am I doing here?"

The question of who we are causes me to look to quantum physics and Vedanta, which is Eastern philosophy. They both say that all of what we are and see comes from a single source, which appears as different forms, much like water, which can appear as steam or as ice while still remaining $H_2O$.

We are really forms made up of common stuff called "being" or "consciousness." Being unfamiliar with that causes us to believe we are separate individuals, unconnected. I say this from only brief experiences of the inner self that we all are, but we could think of life like a movie, which is only illusion, and our consciousness as the screen that allows the show to be seen. But to recognize this intellectually is not enough to satisfy us; we need to know this by being it. Life would still have its changes and ups and downs, but our fulfillment would always be present as the constant serenity of our own being.

This is not anything new; it has been experienced by fortunate people throughout the ages. They have tried to pass this message on to others, and some people listen and learn to live this reality and pass it on to still others. The invitation is open to all. I hope we all see the truth of it as it will lead to fulfillment for all who claim it.

# *Psychosis and Writing on Spiritual Issues*

On rare occasions during severe depressions, people's thoughts can become entwined with spiritual ideas in unusual ways. While you're unlikely to experience this, it is a phenomenon that has been recognized in various cultures for thousands of years and is worth consideration in light of the ways depressed people are treated today.

Psychosis—a state of having hallucinations and/or delusions—does occur on rare occasions for some people during depression as well as in bipolar disorder and schizophrenia. And it's not uncommon for such confused states to involve spiritual themes—seeing God or other spiritual figures, for example. These situations can prove tricky for psychiatrists to handle.

"While some people with mental illness become super-religious and have religious hallucinations and/or delusions, we should not forget that others may also have genuine religious experiences as well,"[4] writes Catholic priest Jerome Stack. How do you treat the symptoms of a very ill person without disrespecting, even shattering, their spiritual beliefs?

In the Western medical system, psychiatry and, in fact, most of the medical profession, have avoided addressing patients' spiritual lives for a long time. Beginning with Freud in the late nineteenth century, there was a general understanding in psychiatry that religious commitment fosters psychopathology and is rarely correlated with good mental health. However, that attitude is beginning to change. In fact, many American residency training programs for new psychiatrists now include instruction on religious and spiritual issues as they may affect people with mental illness.

Can writing in or after a psychotic period help or harm the person? Here's my experience: both during deep depressions and during the occasional manic episodes my illness has brought me, I've sometimes had thoughts about God and the universe that in retrospect, from a healthier state, seem bizarre. For me, these sometimes involved music (for example, believing that if I could only turn a Bruce Springsteen CD up loud enough, I could see, maybe even touch, God, and God would lift me out of my miserable despair). I've been fortunate that while my thinking in some dark times—about music and God, about having cancer when no evidence of such existed, about hearing voices down the hall when no one was home—seems "off," and would be diagnosed as a bit psychotic, it has always eventually resolved itself without harm. Then I've been able to see that while I may have strong spiritual beliefs, they probably don't depend upon loud rock music.

There's no way I could write cohesively during a psychotic period, but what about afterward? I've found that writing about experiences post-psychosis has been very cathartic—and creativity researchers suggest that the creativity of some ill authors and artists has been enhanced by such exploration. Writing has allowed me to record, examine, and gain some validation for just how strange and scary those times can be. And writing down even my temporary beliefs about cranking up the stereo to touch God lets me reflect on what those beliefs might reveal about my everyday views of life.

*We should write because it is human nature to write. . . . We should write because human beings are spiritual beings and writing is a powerful form of prayer and meditation, connecting us both to our own insights and to a higher and deeper level of inner guidance as well.*

—Julia Cameron,
 *The Right to Write*

Writing has definitely helped as I try to place these periodic bizarre events in the context of my illness as a whole, and in my life. I have not seen it harm or unduly upset any of my group members who have had spiritual psychotic experiences in the past. I've sometimes even pondered potential benefits of encountering such rare and peculiar states—can they lend depth to writing I do later? I'm not sure yet how I might use my fleeting visions of a cheetah in the living room in my future writing, but I know that even mentioning it here helps me acknowledge another strange dimension of my experience with depression.

# *Exploring Worlds Within and Without*

Writing can help ease our depression by helping improve our health, our thoughts, our feelings, and our spiritual life. No matter what your beliefs about how the world outside of us operates, or about how our inner worlds work, writing about these things can be fascinating, empowering, and hopeful. It's worth exploring all aspects of our lives in seeking to heal.

## *to write*

### YOUR CHILDHOOD BELIEFS

What spiritual beliefs did you have as a child? Did these come from a religious tradition, your own reflections, or both?

Then consider this: Has your depression affected your spiritual beliefs? How?

### WAITING

In a large or a small sense, what are you waiting for? Are these things affected by your spiritual beliefs?

Here a group member wrote on the topic of "waiting."

### ANOTHER VOICE

*Waiting* by Kerwin J. Lee, M.D.

I wait for the peace away from all those violent dreams that awaken me soaked in sweat. I wait for the quiet of my mind when all that bangs and clashes in my head recedes. I wait as those memories of pain and the pain itself dissolve into a pool of peace. I am waiting and have been waiting for a long time. Sometimes life is so sad, but I can wait, for I believe there is more.

# II.
# WRITE IT OUT

*how to write through*

*the darkness*

# Chapter 6

# *Journaling and Freewriting as You Build Your Writing Habit*

*When I've written for a while I always feel like something inside me has been released. . . . It's amazing how words flow from my subconscious and reveal thoughts and ideas I had no idea existed.*

—CARLA

How many of us have said it? "I want to write, but I just can't find the time . . . can't seem to get started . . . don't know what to write about. . . ." The list goes on and on. . . .

You've already been doing writing exercises in this book as we've discussed depression, authors who've coped with depression, and writing's healing properties. This chapter is where you learn how and why to begin a *habit* of writing regularly—the foundation of all writing—and how to keep it going. We'll discuss two different approaches to a steady writing habit—journaling and freewriting—so that you can learn what works best for you under various circumstances.

*There's a friend at the end of your pen [that] you can use to help you solve personal or business problems, get to know all the different parts of yourself, explore your creativity, heal your relationships, develop your intuition . . . and much more.*

—KATHLEEN ADAMS,
*Journal to the Self*

As you're discovering how to beat the "I-want-to-write-but" blues, you can also consider what topics you most want to write about in order to ease your depression. You may want to hit a discussion of your symptoms head on; you may choose to gradually uncover your feelings about past difficulties; you may work to create a plan for your recovery. And you may want to use your words to simply create for the joy and sense of exploration it offers, and see where it leads you.

## *Journaling: Introspection and Having a Dialogue with Yourself*

Have you ever kept a diary? When I ask this of people in general, depressed or not, I find that most have at some time, however briefly. Keeping a diary typically means keeping a record of events. Some people find them hard to maintain because their content is rather dry. I began writing in a small, pale blue book with a tiny lock and key when I was about six years old. I came across it recently and discovered that I had carefully recorded the daily events of my life and my family's—and that my entries stopped after a whopping six days.

*I have found as much uplifting and awe-inspiring passages in private journals as I have from the "great works" of the acknowledged masters.*

—HAL ZINA BENNETT, *Write from the Heart*

Journaling, on the other hand, is more colorful. It is journeying inside yourself to see what really lies there below the surface. It is crawling on your knees, using an archeologist's brushes to clean off the artifacts of your mind—the memories, ideas, emotions, and plans, be they ancient or recent, fragile or sturdy, simple or ornate.

Your journal is a place to go when you want to retreat from the outside world and converse with yourself. When you're depressed, it is a place to consider the pain of your emotional and physical symptoms, whether they are in response to a recent job loss, a divorce, a long-ago abuse, or a biochemical glitch. You can ask yourself questions and search for the answers in the safety and privacy of pages devoted to your eyes only. Your journal can become a place for describing dreams—the ones that fill your sleeping brain and the daytime ones that dare to peek out at an uncertain future. You can plan how you want to get well again, the new job you'll find then, and the old relationship you'll heal from. Writing in a journal can calm and soothe you, heal and reorganize you.

In addition to journaling on your own, there are various types of more formal "journal therapy," which can provide "structure, pacing and containment"[1] according to Kathleen Adams, director of the Center for Journal Therapy; see the resources section in her book *The Way of the Journal* (Sidran Institute Press, 1998).

Whether writing individually or in a therapy context, you can grow within the pages of your journal, too. You'll find answers you didn't know you had for questions that have been plaguing you. And you'll find questions that you hadn't even realized were gnawing at you. As a result, you'll change. You'll become a different person. As hard as it can be to recognize when we're deep in its throes, depression is a growing experience—usually a signal that something is seriously awry in our life—and journaling provides a means to reckon with these situations. Through writing, we can also learn how to live with our depression, to manage our symptoms, to have the faith to try new approaches to healing, and to prioritize our activities, since we may not be able to spread our energies as we once could. And by writing, we can learn to hope—to believe that things will improve, that life still offers rewards. In your journal you will record, ponder, analyze, interpret, review, learn about, and, ultimately, act upon your life with depression.

I recently did some of these things as I journaled on the topic of depression itself.

> "Depression." It defines my life. I hate it. Miserable depression. Most people don't have to experience it, which is good, of course, but it makes it so much harder for them to understand what I'm going through. I'm so alone, like I'm the only one in the world who has ever felt this deeply sad, hopeless, paralyzed. Sometimes I'm sure I'll never get better. Thankfully, I have Mary, my friend, who is bipolar too. I complain to her when I feel helpless and doomed. Yesterday, after I described my mood crash from okay to total despair, where I want to crawl in a hole and not do

anything, I felt a bit better. Not well, but better. She has really been in the abyss before too. Low, where she thought she'd never get well. She reminded me that I'm not the lazy fool wasting my life that my inner critic voice had been saying.

One caveat: make sure you're moving forward with your healing as you write in your journal. Don't ruminate endlessly on the same old problem in the same old way every time you write—this obsessive overanalyzing does not help and, according to research studies, might actually be harmful.[2] If you don't feel you're progressing in your understanding and processing of the issue, try some of the other techniques described in this book and mix in other topics. If you still feel stuck, it's probably a good idea to consult a professional mental health care provider.

## *to write*

### AN INTERNAL CHALLENGE

**Allow yourself to go inside and explore deeply as you journal about a personal emotional challenge you've faced in your life. It may be something small, like losing a third-grade spelling bee, or larger, like coming to terms with a breakup. How did you feel at the time? How did you cope with the emotions of that trial?**

In this excerpt, group member Kate V. explored the emotional challenge of accepting her diagnosis of bipolar disorder.

### ANOTHER VOICE

### *The Most Mysterious Thing* by Kate V.

This new understanding of myself really means opening up to the greater unknowns. What combination of treatments and new tools—medications, therapies, diet, exercise, sleep—will help me find a better balance? How does one even know when things are working well, or is that a silly question? How does one sift through all the disparate selves and identify with a single personality? I just feel disoriented, like I am trying to see my reflection in a mirror but must look though an old unfocused pair of binoculars so that I cannot see all of me, just two blurry and fractured images jumping in and out of focus, the two images refusing to overlap to reveal my whole self. I'm a mystery even to myself and I don't know how to decipher it.

## *"Freewriting"—What Does It Mean?*

After I'd journaled for several months and felt its power, I began to further explore writing. I've always been a reader. Reading is often my first way of investigating and learning about the world, so I naturally turned to the library and the bookstore to see just what had been written about writing itself. I was fortunate that one of the first books I happened to get my hands on was *Writing Down the Bones* by Natalie Goldberg (Shambhala, 1986). I fell in love with it. I read Natalie's other books, including *Wild Mind* (Bantam, 1990); I even eventually studied writing with her at two different workshops in Taos, New Mexico, where she lives. And these are still the first books I recommend to students beginning to explore the world of writing.

Goldberg, who began studying Zen Buddhism as a young adult, followed her spiritual path by developing a *writing practice*—a regular habit of doing what other writers and teachers also call *freewriting*—as a means of exploring the mind, akin to meditation. In freewriting, you typically start from a writing prompt, a topic or question or word, and write continuously on it for a given amount of time. For example, I might begin a writing session with ten minutes on "my kitchen." Of course, my writing topic may evolve from my microwave to my memory of the smell of Mom's spaghetti sauce simmering on the stove when I was young; this is fine.

I see freewriting as an approach that differs from but also overlaps with journaling. As Goldberg describes it in *Wild Mind*, "Journal writing seems to be about thought, about rumination and self-analysis. One of the rules of [free] writing practice is, Don't think. We want to get below discursive thought to the place where . . . [t]houghts just arise impersonally from the bottom of our minds."[3]

Now there's nothing wrong with the thought and self-analysis of journaling—I believe journaling holds an important place among writing techniques. However, I suggest you experiment with the freewriting approach as well. It will give you another tool with which to explore writing. I think you'll find that while journaling, you tend to write about yourself to yourself and gain insight into your thoughts and feelings; with freewriting, you're expressing yourself about the whole world, with the result that you investigate and reflect upon both yourself and the rest of the world. One helps you make inner connections; the other, outer connections.

Today there are times I want to focus on me, my life, my feelings—and then I journal; there are other times I freewrite to change my point of view and begin to explore the rest of the world in my words. Both are wonderful, and my writing group members and I have found both very fruitful when delving into different aspects of our emotions and moods. Also, writers write with different techniques on different days or when in different moods. So experiment and see which is most useful to you and when.

When you're freewriting, you'll write intensely, quickly, and with depth. Freewriting is what I usually encourage people to use in creative writing groups. One reason is that it stimulates them to try something different than the journaling they may have started doing at home. Furthermore, freewriting is the beginning of creating art and exploring other forms of writing—telling stories from your life or your imagination, putting fictional endings on them to see how they feel, crafting poetry, and developing ideas that you'll communicate to others.

When I freewrite, I do feel a different kind of power. I feel in touch with the universe, not just my own mind. And I find that the tone and voice of my freewriting does differ somewhat from my journaling, too. This is what appeared when I decided to freewrite on the same topic I used for journaling above—depression.

"Depression." What a word. There used to be the word "melancholia" for this state, but I guess I'd sound a little crazy (!) using this term today. "Melancholy," its relative, does imply an emptiness to me. That's how depression feels, all right—like I'm a hollow shell, empty inside. I wonder sometimes exactly how others experience their depression—but we can never truly feel what another feels; we can only imagine. We can only compare what our doctors say, or how we rate on those depression inventory surveys they use sometimes. It ultimately comes down to what you do with it. Seek the best treatment you can find and fight like a tiger to keep going every day. The people I know who have eventually fared the best have also reached out to help others when they were able.

It's important to note that you could freewrite or journal on this topic hundreds of times and get hundreds of different pieces of writing. We are different people every time we approach the page. However, as I look at these two excerpts, I do find that the journal entry was more focused on my internal ruminations, while the freewriting was more patient and free-ranging and connected to the world, although it was still about my opinions and feelings.

## *to write*

### AN EXTERNAL LIFE CHANGE

Think of a life change you have faced that has changed your external as well as your internal life. It may have been a move, a marriage, the death of someone close, an illness, or a job change, for example. As you freewrite, describing it on paper, consider this: Did it change any later decisions you made? Did it change any relationships for you? In what ways have you integrated it into your present life?

Here a writing group member described a major external change in his life.

### The Death of a Loved One by Kerwin J. Lee, M.D.

My mother was a hard person to love. Things were great when her mood was stable, but when she was manic or depressed she was hard to love . . . or at least her moods were hard to love. Looking back, even when I thought I could love her in all of her moods and her decline to death, it was not to be so. The last year of her life she was deeply lost in her dementia, and her heart disease kept on going. I knew from my medical background that she had less than a year to go. During this last year of her life my father wore himself out taking care of her. I thought there would be great peace in her passing. Well, it was not that way when she died. My father was filled with remorse for not being at her bedside in the hospital at the moment of her death. He still talks about his regret. He has a strong faith that Mother is in a better place, that in due time he will join her. His faith tempers his remorse.

I, on the other hand, wonder in what sort of place she may be, and in my doubt my feelings fragment and fly in all directions. My hate and anger are right there next to the love and affection I felt for her. I feel lost when I try to sort out my feelings. Even worse, my severe depression triggered by Mother's death led me to twelve ECTs (electroconvulsive therapy treatments) in one month, and to a place . . . a slippery place where names, faces, and past events have moved to uncertainty. I continue to go once a month for one ECT as "maintenance," so they say, to keep my mood stable. However, I cannot remember things and I remain unable to work. All of this comes from my mother's death. While I love her dearly I still feel so angry about what has happened since her death.

# Developing Your Writing Habit

You've been writing periodically as you've completed exercises in the preceding chapters. Now it's time for the next step: increase your healing power by using freewriting and journaling techniques to start writing frequently, on a schedule. The first big question for most beginners is, "Just how much time do I need to set aside for writing to ease depression?" Not all that much, to start, so quiet that voice in your head that just began to tell you how busy you are and how you'll never find time for one more activity in your day. I feel that ten or twenty minutes a session—the amount of time you're using to write exercises in this book—is a fine place to start. If you end up writing for four hours, terrific, but don't feel you need to set aside huge blocks of time. Keep it simple to start.

*"[W]rite every day for a little while," my father kept saying. . . . "Do it by pre-arrangement with yourself. Do it as a debt of honor."*

—ANNE LAMOTT, *Bird by Bird*

More important than writing for long stretches is writing regularly, that is, every day, or at least several days a week. It's like getting physical exercise—a half-hour, three or four times a week is better than just one long workout on Sunday. There are several reasons for trying to write frequently. One delight you'll find as you begin to write regularly is that your writing gets better—quickly. As you get used to the familiar feeling of opening your notebook or sitting down at your computer to write, your writing voice will become freer and stronger. It will become more specific, more descriptive and detailed, more expressive, more characteristically "you." Instead of editing yourself as you painstakingly put down each word, you'll be creating sentences and exploring ideas fluidly. You'll find you can access memories, thoughts, and feelings more readily, too. I find, as do the frequent writers in my group, that these more flexible thought patterns are the most helpful for investigating and alleviating depressed feelings.

Surprisingly, research hasn't officially weighed in one way or another yet on the benefits of daily writing. "Ironically, there is no clear evidence that keeping a daily journal or diary is good for your health,"[4] writes research psychologist James W. Pennebaker in *Writing to Heal* (New Harbinger, 2004). Still, the anecdotal evidence of the benefits of writing regularly is plentiful.

Most professional writers seem to have their own rules about how much and how often they write. Some write for three hours straight without question, while others adhere to producing a specific number of words every day. Julia Cameron, author of *The Artist's Way* (Tarcher/Putnam, 1992) and other creativity books, advocates that everyone write "Morning Pages"—filling three pages with writing immediately upon waking.

The most important reason for developing a regular writing habit may be momentum. Writing begets more writing. It's very easy to fall into the trap of *thinking* about writing more than actually writing, and soon you're not, in fact, committing anything to the page. As long as you are writing, you are a writer. You can take pride in that. But just imagining what you want to write about isn't enough—you'll easily lose those ideas if they're not recorded, and, even more crucially, you'll lose out on all the unique and healing thoughts and feelings that putting them on paper would have triggered. You'll discover some wonderful surprises that come up when you write that don't seem to arise in any other way. I am frequently amazed how, when writing about a vexing, discouraging problem, a simple solution or a complete change of attitude appears on the page. So don't lose those treasures—write, and write frequently, to keep up your momentum.

If you do lose momentum, you can easily forget how much writing can help you feel better. We all tend to lose track of this, but when we're depressed, that connection can evaporate even more easily. In order to write steadily several days a week, you may need to specifically schedule writing time on your calendar or place it on your to-do list or make a date with yourself or with a friend to write. And if you blow it, if you just haven't been able to coax yourself to sit down and pull out your pen for a while? Start over. Start fresh and you'll soon build some momentum for yourself again. Don't let that notebook grow dusty as you chastise yourself, which depression may lead you to do. Be kind to yourself and just start over. Be a writer.

## Finding What Heals You

At times, I find that either journaling or freewriting can take me to another state—one like I've felt in meditation, when I have no idea how much time has passed. I'm almost unaware of making these tiny movements with my fingers, hardly conscious of the words I'm putting down, until a sudden luminous insight or an almost-lost memory appears in my mind and I jerk to awed attention. That's when I remember how I love to write, to create something unique in all the world. If that doesn't help me heal, what could?

Still, I know it's not easy to get there, especially when I'm deeply depressed. In the next chapters, we'll discuss several types of writing so that you can experiment to discover what most interests and most heals you. We'll consider poetry, memoir, fiction, and sharing your writing—with those close to you or with the public. Finally, we'll discuss ways to *use* your depression as you express yourself in writing, how to choose what to write about when your mind is dragging a bit, and techniques to help you keep on writing through the ups and downs.

*to write*

### SOLITUDE

Personally, I need alone time—sometimes a lot of it. It keeps my mood more stable, my stress level lower, and I can be more creative. But I understand from some people that for them, a lot of solitude isn't necessary.

Do you embrace being alone or merely tolerate it when it occurs? Do you feel invigorated or lonely? If lonely, does it pass quickly or does it linger and feed depression?

# Chapter 7

# *Poetry to Light the Darkness*

*Whenever I get somewhere, a poet has been there first.*

—Sigmund Freud

Many writers have naturally turned to poetry as an outlet for the painful thoughts and feelings of depression as well as for their observations of the world around them. In this chapter, we'll consider how and why the intensity and immediacy of poetry can often help the writer express and process difficult emotions. For some of us, poetry flows easily and is even a preferred mode of writing. However, I've also known writing group members to protest, "But I don't know how to write poetry!"

As we read examples of poetry on depression and hope, this chapter will ask, "What is poetry?" It will then offer ideas and exercises to help you gently start to write your own poems. This can be an especially healing genre of writing to explore. Even if you usually prefer to write prose, you may want to give poetry a try.

## *Poetry Is Different and Powerful*

You might be someone who compulsively scribbles daily poems about your life events and emotions as a means of processing and healing, or you may have been one in the past—many adolescents use poetry for self-expression. On the other hand, you may be glad that you haven't had to look at a poem since elementary school. If you fall into the latter category, perhaps you also remember only singsongy rhymes telling children how to behave—

or else. If you studied any poetry in later school years, you may still feel the annoyed confusion of trying to understand the "thees" and "thous" of romantic poetry. But poetry is much more than those forms and topics, and it does have great relevance in the twenty-first century and in the life of those coping with difficult emotions.

Poetry is simply a different, and powerful, type of writing. It is accessible to everyone—fear not! So what makes poetry special? Here are three things that help distinguish poetry:

- Many types of poetry are relatively short, which can add a sense of urgency and focus to the meanings of poems.

- Poetry is compact; no unneeded words are used.

- Poetry pays special attention to the rhythm and sounds of the words used, including rhymes.

Because of these characteristics, we naturally recognize poetry when we hear it—a poem sounds different than *prose* (writing in regular sentences, as in freewriting or journaling). And when we read it, we see that it looks different on the page, too.

Poetry has been written in many different "forms" over the ages, each making different use of those rhythms and sounds. For example, you've perhaps heard of the three-line poetic form known as *haiku*. This ancient type of Asian poetry, usually written about the natural world, is very precisely organized. It requires five syllables in the first line, seven in the second, and five in the third. *Sonnets*, such as Shakespeare's, comprise another form, written under different but also demanding rules: fourteen lines, composed in the iambic pentameter metering scheme, with exacting rules for which line must rhyme with which.

*Poetry is a natural medicine; it is like a homeopathic tincture derived from the stuff of life itself—your experience.*

—JOHN FOX, *Poetic Medicine*

You may be relieved to know that most poetry written today is in *free verse*, which doesn't require any rhyming or special meter or line length. This is the type of poetry we'll discuss in the remainder of this chapter—though you are of course encouraged to explore more formal forms on your own.

Although there are no rules about the rhythm of the syllables and words in free verse, and the poet has complete control over where each line *breaks* (where one line ends and the next begins), both of those poetic "devices" are still important for the poet to consider consciously. Of course, the process of choosing precisely the right words—vivid, sensual, evocative ones—is very important, too. In good prose, every word is important and necessary; in good poetry the same is true, and vague or unneeded words tend to stand out even more. Don't let yourself become immobilized as you try to think of the

> *When you are composing a verse, let there be not one hair's breadth separating your mind from what you write. Quickly say what is on your mind; never hesitate a moment.*
>
> —Basho, fifteenth-century Japanese poet

"right" word for each line of your poetry, but let your mind and heart go and your intuition will likely lead you to them. And remember, after you've written a whole first draft of a poem, you can always go back and make changes and improvements.

Poetry often uses other special devices too, which help distinguish it from prose. These include strong imagery (which describes any physical sensation, not just visual), similes ("My depression arrives *like* an ocean wave") and metaphors ("My depression *is* an ocean wave"). But don't worry—you already naturally use many of these devices when you write and speak. In fact, as you've been writing in response to exercises in this book, you've probably already used some. Rather than attempting to explain poetic devices in detail, this chapter will focus on approaches and exercises that have proven healing for me and for other members of my group. One excellent book that can help teach and guide you if you would like to further explore the world of poetry and healing is *Poetic Medicine* by John Fox (Tarcher/Putnam, 1997). Other very good guides to writing poetry are listed in the *Bibliography and Selected Resources* section.

# Getting Started

The following exercises offer some poetry topics and some ideas about how you might approach them. I often begin writing a poem by noting any images that come to my mind right away when I think of that subject. (Remember,

we'll use the term "image" to refer to a physical detail coming from *any* of the senses.) I also note the emotions I have around the topic and think of what images they trigger. Then I try to write quickly, intuitively, putting down the words that feel right to me and arranging them on the page in a way that feels natural. Often these first thoughts and feelings are the deepest and truest, and I want to capture them while they are fresh rather than worrying prematurely about correcting or fixing them. And I try to remember to have fun! Writing poetry can be very free-ing, like when your prose writing begins to flow for you.

## *to write*

### PLAYING WITH LINE BREAKS

What does your depression look like? Is it a hole in the earth, a monster, a swamp? And how does it sound, smell, taste, and feel? Look back at what you wrote on this topic in chapter 2 or jot down a few images now. Write a poem with these images by arranging your words and phrases into lines of free verse, paying attention to where the lines break. See what feels natural to you and how you can play with the sound and look of the lines, and even use them to change the emphasis of the words.

In this exercise, in response to the prompt, "How Do You Picture Your Depression?" one group member imagined herself "sitting in a chair staring straight ahead, heavy headed and spaced out." From this image, she wrote this poem. Notice how she broke up the lines to create a slight pause between certain words and phrases.

**ANOTHER VOICE**

### *Picture of Depression* by Jo Bobbie

The chair sits in a forest
Rain dripping down
My thoughts move sloth-like
Down the tree trunks
Pulling back my head
Heavy damp black feelings slumber by
I can hear the muffled choking
In the distance; not a surprise
It's been going on for too long
Dark slow feelings, castrated happiness
Not to be captured by my fingers
Or eyes blinking by.
Forget about it.

# *Healing with Poetry*

Poetry therapist Nicholas Mazza, who studies the ways the poetic form can assist with disabling emotions, reports in his book *Poetry Therapy* (Brunner-Routledge, 2003) that both writing poems and responding to those you read can help clarify and focus your thoughts, provide catharsis, and offer a means of expressing your feelings. Let's focus next on communicating your feelings by considering a safe, calming image.

> *to write*
>
> ## A HEALING IMAGE
>
> Sit quietly for a moment and imagine the most soothing image you can—one that might counter your depression. Is it a place? A person? The feel of the breeze? A special remembrance? Write a poem describing it and, again, use as much sensory detail as possible.

In this poem, Heather described what was a healing image for her—the ritual of burning papers on which she had written old hurts.

**ANOTHER VOICE**

### *A Healing Image* by Heather Tolles

> A violet flame:
> Cauterizing the wounds,
> Purifying the unclean,
> Leaving golden ashes—
> Fertilizer for
> The budding soul.

## *Facing Down Depression in Poetry*

Taking on the topic of your depression in the direct manner of poetry can sometimes be intimidating. On some days you may feel emotionally ready to approach it head on; on other days, not. Consider some of these options for writing poetry about depression: Choose one aspect of your depression, such as insomnia, and write about it specifically and then relate it to the whole issue of depression at the end of the poem. Or, starting with "I feel . . .," write a litany of your symptoms in the form of a poem to your doctor or therapist, using just one line for each symptom. Or, as in the exercise below, write *to* your depression about your relationship with it.

## A LETTER TO DEPRESSION

**What would you like to say to your depression? Write a poem in the form of a letter to it.**

In the following poem, I wrote an open letter to my depression, telling it that it does not escape my notice, even when it tries, and lamenting that I can't escape its notice either.

### To Depression

Ghostlike, you watch me in my morning shower.
You hover in the corner of the kitchen.
You sit seductively on the soft sofa
Wearing an evil smirk,
Beckoning for me to spend
My precious hours there with you.
I feel you beside me
As I drive down 101
Doubting anyone has ever loved me.
And at the cocktail parties you delight in,
You dress up and slip between people
To poison my chardonnay.
You always find me easily,
Though I scramble from you like my timid cat
Who dives under a flat bedspread,
Thinking her lump invisible.
But I also fight your clever attacks!
I gobble pills like M&Ms.
I let people hold magnets and electrodes
To my head, slip needles into my scalp.
And you skulk away for days or weeks.
Still, you spy, and when I start to relax,
You return in the night to watch me sleep
And swaddle me in your web of grief.

# More Poetry Subjects

Poetry can be written about nearly any topic. A great deal of poetry has been written about nature, for example, and emotions have also constituted the focus of much poetry over the centuries as well as today. For many people, poetry seems to be a unique and direct way of accessing feelings and thoughts and working through them as if solving a puzzle.

## *to write*

### A LIST OF TOPICS

Take a few minutes and quickly write a list of topics you would like to explore in your poetry. These may include concrete items, like your pet or the tree outside your window as it changes colors in autumn, as well as less tangible items like love or depression.

Choose one topic and write a list of words or images related to it, keeping them as detailed and sensory as possible—be specific rather than general. Now use this second list to create a poem that either describes or makes a comment on the original topic. This list-making approach is a good one to return to when you have a topic in mind but aren't sure where to go with it.

### THE TOPIC OF WRITING

Reflect on why you write. What made you pick up this book? In what ways do you find writing healing to you? Compose a poem about this activity itself.

The following group member wrote a poem about writing and how it helps her cope with her bipolar disorder. Like several other writers in our group, English is not her first language, and she finds poetry a particularly accessible form.

*How Writing Helps* by Helen Han

> So messy room in my brain
> Too dirty things in my heart
> So many memories in my mind.
> But if I hold a pen and write something on
> The paper, the messy, dirty many memories
> Find the way out.
> Soul
> Spirit
> Connecting with a good friend to hear well
> And talking is good, too.
> But if I have time to write, it's better.
> God's help.

# Reacting to Past Experiences

As in writing prose, looking back at difficult experiences and writing our thoughts and feelings about them helps us process those events. Sometimes the painful events have helped trigger our depression; sometimes the painful event is living with our mental condition itself.

## to write

### REFLECTING ON THE PAST

Recall an emotional experience you've been through, whether it was painful, joyous, shocking, angering, or elicited some other strong feeling. Write a poem that includes how it felt at the time and how you think and feel about it today. Has your perspective grown broader over time? Does that time of your life now hold new meaning for you?

This poem, by a member of our group, looks back at a difficult emotional period, a manic phase of bipolar disorder. Notice how Robert used images and mixed up the words in some lines to illustrate the disorganized way his mind felt. At the end, he considered his place relative to the larger world.

**ANOTHER VOICE**

### *Ruins* by Robert Voss

Small and Quiet I
At epicenter
Of a bygone quake
Smoking in the ruins

Fivefold aftershocks
Scattered my Reason
Shifting reality
Becoming my cell

Do you want to know
Thinking what I this
Of creation made
With parts rearranged

Feeling lonely cold
Afraid of before
Becoming again
It just might break me

Shifting in the ruins
I seek Eternity
Knowing I will fail
But needing the stance

After we have looked back at an experience and described and processed it emotionally, we can turn to the larger issues of how and why it occurred. In the following poem, I wondered why I happened to be a person with depression and considered whether there had been some spiritual "bargaining" that had taken place.

### I Didn't Sign Up for This

The Universe chose this path for me.
I don't know why.
Perhaps I bargained
Before I was born—
Suffocating emotions,
Suicidal yearnings,
In exchange for
Four working limbs,
No breast cancer,
No heart attacks at age forty.
Or maybe I did choose this route
For reasons now evaporated
From memory—
To witness the mind's oddities?
Fight prejudice?
Walk a new life path?
I try to weigh these things.
But when life-sucking
Rolls of white gauze
Wrap around me,
Stilling my muscles,
Numbing my thoughts
But not the searing pain
In my chest,
I think those reasons are not enough.
No. I didn't sign up for this.

## *Poems in Response to Poems*

While you've been writing poetry in response to prompts in this chapter, another aspect of using poetry to help heal ourselves is to appreciate the inspiration we can get from the poems of others. I often use a favorite poem—or one brand new to me—to spring forward with my own writing of either poetry or prose. Often the vivid sensual images of poetry trigger deep new images of my own. Possible approaches include the following: writing in response to the ideas or observations in the poem; choosing one line, one phrase, one word, or one image, and using it as a prompt; or writing a letter to the poet in response to the poem. So consider these uses of poetry, too, as you learn which kinds of writing feel most healing to you. The exercises in chapter 14 suggest numerous poems you might enjoy responding to, and the *Bibliography and Selected Resources* section offers several books that are good places to continue exploring poems and poetry.

# Chapter 8

# *Writing Your Life in Memoir*

Dear Julie,

I'm sitting and watching the spray of a huge fountain on campus at 8:30 in the morning. Hardly anyone's around yet, but I need to tell someone that I just saw a psychiatrist and he thinks I have clinical depression. My chest tightened as he said it. I'm terrified this means I'm on a slippery slope toward crazy.

I guess depression would explain my crying spells every time I see a sentimental ad on TV, and why I truly dread getting up and going in to the lab each morning. I don't think I hate graduate school; it's more that something's wrong with me. Something's strange.

I'm going to start taking antidepressant medication, which is scary. But it also makes me wonder a lot (you know me, the biologist)—how are the chemicals in this little pill supposed to change my thinking and my emotions? And why do I need to take a stupid pill to make my mood normal anyway? Shouldn't I be able to do that myself?

Thanks for letting me vent.

Love,

Beth

We all write memoir when we write a letter or an e-mail telling of our lives. I pulled this letter out of the book-length memoir of my bipolar disorder that I am completing. Looking back, I can now see that the process of writing the tale of my illness changed me dramatically. My self-image evolved; events and emotions were processed and integrated; I developed a new, more positive worldview in light of even sometimes miserable experiences.

Though writing a memoir was painstaking, I highly recommend the project for any writer—and telling their story is a common desire among numerous writers I know who are coping with depression. Many of us instinctively feel this can be a healing endeavor.

This chapter will discuss writing about your experiences with depression in the form of a detailed story and will help you take the first few steps.

## What Is a Memoir?

First of all, let's get our terms straight. What is a memoir? Is it the same as an autobiography? And what does it mean when someone has "written her memoirs" (plural)?

Let's begin with *autobiography*. This refers to a story of a person's entire life, written by that person. The *biography* is analogous—a story of someone's life written by another author. Having "written one's memoirs"—an old-fashioned term—typically means that a person has written an autobiography. However, the term is generally used by politicians, movie stars, and the like, and often anecdotes about other well-known people or events are included. By contrast, a *memoir* is more specific, framing the author's remembrance of a *particular aspect* of her life during a particular time. (Note that "memoir" and "memory" come from the same root.)

A memoir may be a few pages long or a book-length work. Whether long or short, it will need to have both a theme and a time frame, as we'll discuss further below. For now, consider that your memoir might encompass the story of your painful early childhood or your college love life or your thirty years practicing as a trial attorney or the story of your depression, for example. Other aspects of your life will of course come into play, but they will not become the focal point of the story.

Memoirs have been written about a wide variety of diseases, mood disorders among them. Some of the best contemporary memoirs on depression are William Styron's *Darkness Visible* (Random House, 1990), Marsha Manning's *Undercurrents* (HarperSanFrancisco, 1994), and the memoir portions of *The Noonday Demon* by Andrew Solomon (Scribner, 2001). Kay Redfield Jamison's *An Unquiet Mind* (Knopf, 1995) eloquently describes her bipolar disorder. Reading these, you'll discover that the specific approaches and time spans these books use vary considerably. My own memoir covers the period from shortly before I was diagnosed with a mood disorder to—after several hops and leaps—twenty years later, the time I felt stable enough to move my life forward more steadily again.

## Reasons to Write Your Memoir

Who hasn't at some time finished a book or walked out after a movie and mused, "My life could be a story, too"? I know I've thought, "My life has all the drama, all the twists and turns, all the intense characters of that story—couldn't someone write about *me* or make a film about *me*?" If you have such feelings, it's probably because you sense that there is a real tale to be told. Whether we've formally studied literature or not, I think we all have a certain sense of what makes a good story. After all, we've been hearing or reading fairy tales and ghost stories since we were very young. We know when a story feels compelling and, like hearing a joke with no punch line, we sense when something is off. Looking at your experiences with depression, you may feel something click; something feels right. There's a difficulty, or many difficulties, and there's some sort of resolution. There's a story there.

Paul, like numerous members of the writing group at Stanford over the years, recently announced, rather shyly, that he wished to write a memoir of his illness. He had a tentative but proud, slightly defiant look in his eyes as he said this to the group. Paul felt that not only was there something to be told but also that exposing it would feel satisfying in a way he couldn't quite define. I think Paul sensed that claiming his story would let him say, "Here I am. With all that has happened to me, all that I've done, I am a person worthy of being seen by the world. I am okay." Writing your story may be a powerful way for you too to emotionally "own" and understand even harrowing experiences for yourself.

Though it's not a requirement, many writers set out to pen their memoir specifically so they can share it with certain people. Jesse, for example, writes so her children will know more about her life. Others write in response to people who have made them feel stigmatized. Still others write for their broader family, for others with depression, or for the world at large. Several members of the group have been encouraged by their psychiatrists to write their stories, and these writers may focus on putting words together for that reader who has given them confidence.

For me, writing a memoir of my illness was useful for another reason, too: I felt a desperate need to create something positive out of what was sometimes a horrific experience. At times that thought—that there might be another side to this suffering if I could only grasp it—was what helped me persevere when I was seriously depressed. Developing the writing group I founded was one way to make "something good" happen as a result of my depression; my memoir was another. I wrote it both to claim for myself the story I saw in my experiences and hopefully to provide some insight or comfort for others who might recognize something of their story in mine. These projects have, in fact, given me some relief. Perhaps those difficult years where I felt I did little but survive from one doctor's appointment to the next really did have some value.

*to write*

## WHY WRITE A MEMOIR OF YOUR DEPRESSION?

Describe what intrigues you about creating a memoir and how it might feel to write for those reasons. For example, do you want to show your family just how hard your illness has been on you? Do you want to "make sense of it all" for yourself so that you can move on? Are you driven by feelings of anger, sadness, disillusionment, hope? Then consider, would it feel liberating to write your story? Would it feel comforting? How would it affect your writing process to know that your friends and family could

read what you're writing? There are no right or wrong answers to these
questions, but the answers may help you better understand what is driv-
ing you toward this project and thus help you focus your tale.

## Changes Memoir Writing Can Bring

Looking back, some part of my mind began to nurture a tiny idea about
writing a memoir twenty years ago when I sat and composed that letter to
my friend Julie. That day, in my shock over my diagnosis, I began in some
sense to be "outside" myself. For the first time, I saw my life as something
to observe as well as to live. Teasing the story out of my years of depressions, occasional manic moments, crazy thoughts, and varied treatments
was tougher than I had originally imagined. But like Paul, I also felt a powerful need to make this saga mine. It included sickness, confused realities,
and struggle against death; it involved searching for a passion, a path; and it
described my fear of others' reactions to my travails. I began to realize that
going forward in my life without composing it would be difficult; I *had* to
write my story.

You, too, may be feeling that pull to write your own story. If so, be
prepared for the possibility of a wild ride. One of my surprises as I began
writing about my despair and grief was that impressions and feelings from
my past came up indiscriminately. Indeed, as I slowly put down words,
facts arose that I had forgotten or repressed. Associations appeared that I
had never noticed before. Some of these were happy, but I also had to face
things that I really would have preferred to keep out of my conscious mind.
As they came up, I had to work to digest these thoughts and emotions more
than in any psychotherapy I've experienced.

Memoir writing can change your overall understanding of your illness
too, as you put together the puzzle pieces of your experiences. Through the
writing process, you'll have to integrate the disparate happenings of your
life into a cohesive story in your own mind before you can shape it for

others. As I wrote, I wondered what pieced-together picture of my life I would end up with. Among the fragments I uncovered was my deep sadness at the absence of the career I had hoped for, because for years I had often been too ill to work. My husband and I hadn't had children, as we had expected, because of our concerns about managing a family along with my illness. Finally, I had to look at how close I had sometimes felt to suicide. Writing forced me to remember how at times it felt nearly overwhelming to face the depression's pain.

There can be wonderful rewards from your project as well. In my case, by integrating the events of my life, especially my illness, I am able to see that I really did make it through some horrific times. Looking back on certain chapters, I feel like a proud survivor. You might realize, for example, that you have been brave, stalwart, or generous while weathering your own storms.

Looking back through your memoir-writing process, you'll also see how you've changed. In fact, chances are that your health has improved at least somewhat if you are considering this writing project. I was thrilled when I could see that I had recovered to a great extent. Today I am healthier in many ways—my depressions, and the visions and voices I experience, are less frequent and less severe now, and I have nearly no mania or hypomania. Writing also let me see that when my feelings do start to slip, I'm now better equipped to manage them. I have a greater number of supportive people around me, more flexibility in my responses, a reasonably stable cocktail of medicines, and other treatments. You'll want to consider all the various kinds of life changes that have occurred during the time period you choose.

You may also find that writing your memoir allows you to transcend your illness's effects in some ways. By breaking my history down and examining the important parts, I found I could see what was there; by integrating these things in my mind, I could see what mattered. As a result, I could ultimately see some of the new directions I wanted to take my life in the future.

Finally, writing, and struggling with it day by day and line by line, taught me one of my most treasured life skills: stepping back and just writing. It taught me to write deeply, intensely, and quickly, and to sometimes find the "zone" that I think longtime meditators and serious athletes find. I learned to write freely while still focusing on a specific project. This process of writing from a deep level led me to places I never knew I would go—to ideas, connections, and conclusions I might otherwise not have reached. The sheer delight of this process is no small reward, and indeed it is what leads me to write today. You too may feel that writing calls to you from somewhere deep inside, and creating a memoir may be a very satisfying way to heed that call.

## Starting Your Memoir

A book-length memoir of your depression or bipolar disorder can be a dauntingly long project and can require deep emotional excavation. How can you face this type of work, especially when you're feeling badly? Let's consider ways to begin.

Before you write page one of your memoir, start a notebook just for ideas. As thoughts about the project, memories, and impressions pop into your mind during your day, jot them down right away. Keep the notebook at your bedside at night too, so you can record dreams or other nighttime inspirations that might otherwise get lost by morning. Review your notes every few days and let them trigger additional ideas. These notes may help you discover aspects of your book's theme, remember or arrange scenes, or suggest avenues for freewriting to further explore ideas.

Before you start to turn your notes into writing, it's important to place some limits on the project—remember, this is not an autobiography. Even if you know you want to write about your depression, there are many possible themes to zoom in on. You can describe your symptoms themselves, which may be important, but those symptoms didn't happen in a vacuum. Consider, for example, whether it would be appropriate to approach your depression through its effect on your career, or through your relationship with food or your sex life? When you're depressed, is your lifelong difficult relationship with your father what obsesses you? Did one event, such as the death of a loved one or a traumatic accident, seem to trigger your illness? A theme may appear to you immediately or it may be something that makes itself known only after considerable writing. Still, reflect on the issue now and make notes on your thoughts. This can be an important way to focus your writing process, and it will be crucial to shaping the story as a whole.

*There is no agony like bearing an untold story inside of you.*

—MAYA ANGELOU

You'll also need to delineate your memoir in time. Though you may want to begin and end with the exact dates of your first and last symptoms, consider where in your life history they occurred. You might end up focusing on your childhood years in Alaska, your time working as a chef, or your retirement years. Any of these themes and scopes could create an interesting memoir.

The next step is to break the actual writing into small, manageable pieces. As you make notes about the theme and scope of your story, begin to list the main points of the tale. I found that some of the major points in my memoir included the different treatments I received, my working life during my illness, and my relationship with my husband. Then I broke each of these key ideas down. For example, my treatments included medicines, ECT (electroconvulsive therapy), psychotherapy, acupuncture, and TMS (transcranial magnetic stimulation). Focusing on ECT, I came up with several component parts: what I had heard about ECT from another patient, my first treatment, how I felt after the tenth treatment, and the time I reassured a frightened old woman who was there for her first treatment.

Each of these smaller portions could be written as a scene. A *scene*—a complete set of actions or dialogue—will be one of the key units of your memoir. Scenes can feel manageable because they are relatively short. They can be a great way to approach your writing. It's important to note that a memoir does *not* have to be written in order from beginning to end. You may want to jump around, write the last scene first, the first scene last. For me, it works best to begin with the scene that excites me most as I sit down for a writing session, and then work from there.

*to write*

## GENERATING SCENES FOR YOUR MEMOIR

Close your eyes and take a few deep breaths. Relax and slowly imagine the movie version of your memoir appearing on a screen in front of you, even if your plans for it are still vague. What scenes cross your mind first? Really see them. Allow them to appear, one after the other, for a few minutes. Then open your eyes and take a few more minutes to quickly write a list—as long as possible—of the scenes that you saw. They can be in any order. Some may be very specific, some more general.

Here are some of the scenes on my list: writing the letter while sitting at a fountain, feeling exhausted at my lab bench in grad school, being interviewed when I was hospitalized for the first time, nurses preparing me for ECT, and talking to my friend Louise about my career.

Now read your list and star two or three scenes that contain a lot of physical action. This is the type of scene you'll write first in the next exercise.

As you begin writing, you'll need to examine where the action of the scene really occurs. Start by looking at the scene as an outside observer, as if you are watching yourself on film. For example: *I am alone, cross-legged on a concrete bench. My canvas backpack is beside me, and I stare absently at the falling water in the fountain before me. I pull out a pen and a spiral notebook and begin to write a letter. . . .*

I have found that writing these scenes lets me create portions of my memoir immediately rather than arduously having to figure out where to start each time I sit down to write at the beginning of the project. By carefully saving these scenes in my notebook, I'm holding on to the "jewels" that I'll later string together to make a necklace, along with other types of beads and stones that we'll talk about next. Remember, you don't need to write scenes in order; instead, go where you're drawn and work from there for now.

## *Summary and Reflection*

Writing one scene of your memoir will likely lead you to identify and write more and more. Now you may want to consider the other types of beads that come between the scene jewels on your memoir strand: the *summary* sections and the *reflections* you include. These pieces of writing may occur after most scenes or only occasionally. They can be used to complete or recapitulate a scene or a set of scenes, or they may introduce another piece of the story. Summaries are useful for quickly moving the story along when the next scene is in a different time or place than the last. They vary the pacing of the tale and allow the reader a breather. The very important role of reflection sections is to give you a chance to integrate what's happened so far, to muse about the story. This is where you really get to process the events emotionally and tell the reader how you feel.

Here's an example of a short summary (in italics) that does a little reflecting and then moves the reader forward through time and changes setting:

I finished the letter and stuffed my pen and notebook into my pack.

*That morning had been frightening, yet I felt embarrassed to be making so much of it in my own mind. Thank goodness only Julie knew. An hour later, I was seated on a high stool before my black lab bench, carefully arranging tiny test tubes for an experiment.*

"So, I'm just going to pretend everything is normal today," I thought.

Without a quick summary section, I would have had to write another scene about putting the notebook and pen back in the backpack, standing up, walking across the campus, entering the laboratory building, and sitting down. Since this doesn't sound particularly interesting, the summary lets me avoid it by implying that it occurred. Meanwhile, a little reflection in this summary reminds the reader of Beth's emotional state (frightened) and adds the information that she is now embarrassed as well.

In the next exercise, play with some different ways to summarize and reflect on the scenes you've written.

## to write

### WRITING A SUMMARY SECTION

Choose two of your scenes that occur sequentially and write a connection for them, including your reflections and some summary about how you are moving in time and space. Do you just need to move the story chronologically, or geographically as well? Is this a place in the memoir where you'd like to share with the reader what you think of the events so far? Would this be a good spot to ponder where this personal story will take the narrator in the future? Any of these can make a compelling connection between scenes. This connection might constitute a sentence or be pages in length.

# *Where to Go Next*

A single scene may be many pages long or just a paragraph, but once you've written one, you've begun; your memoir is in progress. So take heart, you're on your way.

As you write more scenes and begin to connect them with summary and reflective material, continue to be attentive to your emotions. As feelings arise in your writing, see whether you can discern what they might mean to your memoir as a whole. Do you find that your hospital visit last summer is the thing that haunts you? Do you get excited about describing how far you've come in your recovery from your depression? Do you realize that you need to do more freewriting about those sad times ten years ago in order to understand their significance for your story? Use these intuitions and emotions to help direct your writing of the memoir *and* to consider as freewriting or journaling topics as well.

As you get more and more of your story down on paper, you'll need to learn about other crucial aspects of a memoir that you'll need to *shape* this string of scenes into a true story. These include choosing which portions of your manuscript to use (you'll likely have to cut some to shape the story) as well as turning to the issues of theme, plot, character development, and other fiction-writing techniques. The more cohesive your story, the more healing it will be for your depression.

As you can see, memoir writing is a big topic. The *Bibliography and Selected Resources* section offers suggestions of several books on memoir to investigate—my favorites include *Becoming Whole* by Linda Joy Myers (Silver Threads, 2003), *Writing the Memoir* by Judith Barrington (The Eighth Mountain Press, 2002), and *Your Life as Story* by Tristine Rainer (Tarcher/Putnam, 1997).

Finally, be aware that just as changes will happen to you, the character in your memoir, changes will occur as you, the author, write about your story, too. Enjoy these as you notice them and emotionally process them. You are likely to uncover new facets of yourself and to grow in self-understanding.

Also, take good emotional care of yourself as you write and remember to pause when you need it. Write deeply, but don't let yourself become depressed by the project itself. You may find that writing your memoir is a very satisfying time as you transcend your history, make sense of it, and come to see yourself as *more* than just the "depressed person" we sometimes feel like.

The following excerpt from the compelling memoir of one of our group members tells of his childhood experiences during the 1956 Hungarian Revolution.

### ANOTHER VOICE

## *The Hungarian Revolution* by George L. Vizvary, Esq.

The Hungary I grew up in was a highly regimented society [in which] daily life and activities were controlled by the Secret Police or the AVO. As an eleven-and-a-half-year-old boy, I could feel the nervousness, and at times terror, of my parents and admired that they tried to give us a different worldview. My sister and I took forbidden English lessons and, probably even worse, were taught the basic precepts of Christianity by a second cousin who was a priest.

In the summer and fall of 1956 there were exciting changes in the air related to the questioning of the dictatorial policies of the Rakosi regime in some open meetings and in the newsprint. When the regime tried to rein in the renegade communists as they had so often in the past, [the renegades] organized a forbidden demonstration for October 23.

During the night of October 22 the students at various universities decided to co-opt the demonstration by pressing for more radical changes; the students invited various labor organizations to join in and many did.

As we sat in class that afternoon a strange noise greeted our ears, and the noise became stranger as the afternoon progressed. At first hundreds and later thousands and then tens of thousands of Hungarians were marching down on Constitution Avenue. What was happening?

The school loudspeaker eventually dismissed us students, with instructions to "go straight home." My sister Kati and my best friend Peter met me in front of the school, and we decided instead to explore the meaning of the day's strange events. But as soon as we reached the hundreds of thousand of people in the square, we became separated.

From that point on I forgot about all else except my desire for the Revolution to succeed. I joined in the cry for Imre Nagy, a renegade communist leader marginalized by Rakosi some years back, to speak, and about 8:00 P.M. he did appear on a balcony of Parliament. He called us comrades, the Communist party salutation, which displeased the crowd and so did the rest of his speech in which he exhorted us to disperse. Then the crowd began to whisper that the Secret Police was holding a gun to Imre Nagy's back, and soon a part of the crowd decided to go to the radio station to have their demands read to the people of the country. I joined in this march.

One of the exhilarating moments of this half-an-hour march was seeing one of my teachers, who a few hours before was lecturing us on the glories of the Soviet Union, shout with the rest of us "Russians go home!"

We reached the building that the radio station was housed in. Soon bullets started whizzing by my head and ricocheting off the building behind me. The Secret Police, which was protecting the building, had fired into the crowd and felled some demonstrators. Soon the ambulances arrived, and the crowd made way for them respectfully so that the wounded could be attended to and the dead could be taken to the morgue. The ambulances did not stop to do their job but went straight to the building housing the radio station, about five hundred feet from where I was standing. Then the crowd, with the sound that only betrayal and perfidy can produce, roared: "The ambulances are full of Secret Police reinforcements!" and started tilting the ambulances until they were upside down, amid a hail of bullets from the building.

Around 11:30 P.M., real reinforcement for the AVO seemed to arrive in a convoy of army trucks loaded with soldiers. This time I was in the front line, but my fear turned into exhilaration as from the truck nearest me the soldiers were handing rifles to the crowd, butt first. Instead of shooting at the crowd, they armed the crowd. At this time I made a fateful decision. As I saw the size of the rifle, I let another pair of eager hands, much larger than mine, grab it and I decided to try to find my way home.

Perhaps an hour later I arrived to find my family and neighbors hysterical with worry for me and my days as a revolutionary were over as my parents put me under "house arrest."

Others carried on!

# Chapter 9

# *Telling Stories: Fiction from Depression*

> *Creativity is an act of survival. It organizes and gives voice to experience.*
> *For creative beings (and we are all creative beings), experience is only*
> *half of an experience. We experience life and then digest it*
> *by making something out of our experience.*
>
> —JULIA CAMERON, *The Vein of Gold*

Writing about our traumas and difficult experiences can help heal our depression—but would you believe that even writing about an imaginary trauma can help? In this chapter we'll explore that concept, and you'll learn the reasons why writing fictitious stories can be healing. You'll also have opportunities to ease into writing some fiction of your own, starting very simply from personal material you've already written.

## *Fiction Is Emotionally Healing*

Knowing that writing about our own traumatic experiences can improve our health, researcher Camille B. Wortman and her team investigated the possibility that writing about traumas that never happened to you could be helpful, too.[1] And surprisingly, it did have significant health benefits. How can this be? It makes sense that writing about our own experiences helps us organize our memories and allows us to develop new perspectives—both healthy things. But apparently writing about the thoughts and feelings we *might* have had as a result of a fictitious event lets us explore feelings we really *have* had in life. For example, you could try writing deeply about experiencing a made-up trauma—say, barely surviving a plane crash—including your reactions and the event's meaning. As a result, perhaps you are tapping into the fear, loss, anger, or hurt that you, like everyone, has experienced at some time—and, suggests researcher James W. Pennebaker, giving those confusing feelings some new meaning.[2]

What exactly is it about writing a fictitious story that is helpful? First let's consider what a story actually is. You already know this intuitively, but it can help to break it down a bit and consider what goes into our favorite book, movie, or fairy tale. We tell stories in the form of *narratives*. That means that there is not just an event but a beginning, a middle, and an end to the story. And this structure usually requires that there is a character who moves through some obstacle to reach a goal. Think of *The Wizard of Oz*, for example. Dorothy, the main character, had the goal of returning home after the tornado, and the whole tale describes how she overcomes obstacles to finally get there. As you develop a story of your own, you'll also automatically create the structure as you choose which events to include and how to shade their meanings. Remember how Dorothy was afraid when meeting the lion but how he became a friend and fellow traveler? Meeting him, and the meaning of how he was friendly and just needed courage, were important choices in moving the story along.

If discussing how stories are created sounds scary at this point, take heart—you already do this all the time! Whenever you tell a friend about how Bob decided to sail around the world or you pass along the gossip of how the neighbor's niece's friend's marriage ended, you naturally create a structure. By giving the story a beginning, a middle, and an end, by describing a character, and by centering the tale around some action, you've made it interesting enough that your listeners will pay attention and even want to know more.

Researchers believe that these acts of creating structure—which also require you to organize emotions and develop some sense of resolution—are healing. By telling stories about difficult events in our lives, we process them in ways that allow us to let go and ruminate less about them. Even when we tell stories that aren't about our own lives, we seem to access that processing power. You may never have seen your house lifted up by a tornado, but you've probably felt fear and loneliness from being away from home. Our minds can use these imaginary scenarios to manage our own disturbing experiences.

As author Pat Schneider puts it in *Writing Alone and with Others* (Oxford University Press, 2003), "Fiction is just another way to tell the truth. And the truths that we have held undisclosed (perhaps even to ourselves) for a long time are under pressure and wanting to come up from the unconscious to the conscious mind. It is the psyche trying to heal itself."[3]

## *Rewriting a Story from Your Life*

One health-promoting approach to writing is seeing an event from a different perspective. There are several ways to do this. One method is to take the story of an experience in your life, which you probably wrote in the first person (using the words "I" or "we") and rewrite it in the third-person perspective (using "he" or "she" or "they"). This gives the feeling that you are outside the event, observing it as it happens to someone else. It offers a new way of looking at what's happening and tends to lead to greater insight into what occurred.

Now let's take that exercise a step further. Take your third-person story and rewrite it, changing one detail that ultimately changes the way the story plays out. Or change the character (originally based on you) in some way that causes the tale's ending to be different. If the taxi had been ten minutes late, perhaps you never would have met Harold, the man who altered the course of your life. If that main character had only been taller, she could have caught the fly ball when the recruiter was watching that day.

*I live with the people I create, and it has always made my essential loneliness less keen.*

—CARSON MCCULLERS, *The Square Root of Wonderful*

Another healing way of creating fiction from your personal memories of a difficult situation is to change the ending of the story in a positive way. For example, if you wrote about your experience of arguing with your boss and then being fired and becoming depressed, change that tale. You could write about disagreeing with your boss, the way he finally agreed with your points, and the promotion you got the next day. This kind of fiction writing from our own lives can be very powerful, and it helps us develop perspective and insight into what really occurred, what we felt about each part of it, and why we have our current feelings about the event.

*to write*

### CHANGING A STORY

**Try changing a story from your life. Choose a difficult life event and take ten minutes to write it as you would any memory, using the first-person (or "I") point of view. Then write the story again, changing the ending so that it resolves in a positive way for you. After writing, consider how you feel and what, if any, insights you gained.**

## Giving Your Feelings Voices

Think for a moment about the different "voices" you hear in your mind at different times—even when you're not depressed. Right now, for example, there may be "Skeptical Voice" saying, "But I don't know how to write fiction!" And perhaps there's "Calming Voice" saying, "Well, let's just keep reading and see if we can learn how to do it." Maybe part of you is raring to go, with "Adventurous Voice" saying, "I can't wait to start—just give me a pen!" One way to begin a story is to develop these different voices into distinct characters and have them talk with one another.

Author Lesley Dormen, writing in *Unholy Ghost* (Perennial, 2001), described how this sort of fiction writing helped her as she was recovering from the worst of her depression: "I found the courage to enroll in a fiction workshop. Now that I could separate out the voices inside my own head, I knew my continued survival depended on the pleasure I felt when I played with them. I began to become a writer."[4]

In the following excerpt, a writer in our group, who copes with bipolar depression, described how creating fictional characters she identified from her dreams has allowed her to listen to and manage her moods.

### ANOTHER VOICE

*Creating Characters* by Diane Warner

At first my writing was a bit like taking notes on books I was reading or just recording some of the everyday things going on in my life. However, as I developed this regular way of starting my days, I also discovered the technique of "self-talk." I took characters from the night's dreams and had them converse on the page. I learned to trust myself to this process because it was private; no one read my journals.

Gradually, I gained confidence in some of the voices that began to grow during these dialogues. One voice was from a lady who lived in a tree and felt she was above everyone else (She actually was!). While I liked her, I felt she was also very distant and removed from earthly matters, so I asked her to come down and start interacting. This very abstract exercise turned out to be a way for me to begin to act differently. This character that I was creating and modifying in written conversations with other internal characters began to be helpful.

In a strange way I was managing my undiagnosed bipolar disorder through writing. It now appears to me that this woman who pretended to be so high and mighty was actually my hypomania. Before I gave her a place, she often "acted out." This was so successful that I decided to give my depressions over to the pen and paper. I began to show myself how down I was about many things and to just allow the feelings a place to talk. Once I started writing from the highs and the lows I could monitor the fluctuations and begin to own the mood swings.

*to write*

## TAKING SILENT DICTATION

Think of a time when you've had ambivalent feelings about a situation, such as a new job offer, a big purchase, or whether to end a relationship. Give a name to each of two or three feelings, and allow these "characters" to talk to each other in your mind. Write for twenty minutes as you simply listen in, taking dictation on their conversation.

## A FABLE OF DEPRESSION

Envision your depression as a living character—one you've never considered before. It might be a Samurai warrior or an evil comic-book character. Then, whatever it is, tell a story about it as if you were telling a simple fable to a small child. Use your intuition and figure the story out as you write. Even when you're not sure it makes sense, amazing tales can appear.

This vivid fairy tale resulted from the prompt, "Give your depression or bipolar disorder a character: What does it look like? What does it say? How does it act?"

### ANOTHER VOICE

### *Dragon* by Robert Voss

The dragon sleeps, yet I am still burned by his somnolent breath. He is in charge of the treasure and postures greedily atop the pile. I dread the times he awakes, for I am chained here in this cave. How did I get here? I used to traipse the verdant green of the valley, until one day my father told me of the dragon in the cave and his hoard of treasure. My father told me to never go there, and I asked him then why did he tell me. He said he wanted me to know there were magical things in the land that were not meant for us. When I asked him how he knew, he told me it was ancient wisdom from the elders.

I was not deterred. I succumbed to an insatiable desire to find the dragon. All the elders said, "Hush, behave" except for the shaman, who told me if I was special I could find the dragon. He told me to search the misty mountaintops, and, thrilled, I began my quest.

After eons, I smelled smoke and trailed its source to a high mountain cave. Excited, I entered the cave and passed through miles of a spelunker's dream. The smell of the smoke grew stronger and stronger until I came upon an ancient hall piled high with gold and gems atop which slept the most beautiful dragon in the world. He was asleep, so I decided to steal a gem. I grabbed too much and the tinkling landslide of treasure awoke the feral beast. With a tremendous snort, he said, "Now you are mine!" and I found myself in chains. I could feel the burn as the dragon played his breath about me. Someday I would like to escape. I felt my error in my treasure lust and the deep pain of knowing I would never be free.

# *Prompts for Your Fiction*

There are an infinite number of other ways to stimulate your fiction writing. When we have just a few minutes left at the end of one of my group's meetings, we sometimes play a "card game" as we sit in our circle around a conference table: each person writes a noun on a note card, passes it one person to the right, and then writes an adjective on a new card and passes it. After three or four words are on each card, the recipient must write a story (not just a sentence) using all of the words. As you can imagine, in some cases this requires a lot of ingenuity, and the results are sometimes hilarious.

You can also start writing fictional stories from virtually any of the writing prompts used in chapter 14 and other parts of this book. Begin with a single word or phrase (for example, "antique watch," "daisy," "campfire song," "a noise in a dark alley"). Or create a character based upon a person in a photograph or painting. Start with a collection of three random objects and write a story that includes all three. And consider interesting situations from which you might write—these can be found in books and on websites (see *Bibliography and Selected Resources* section), or create your own by choosing elements from articles in today's newspapers. In any of these situations, you can be the main character or you can create another protagonist. Set your imagination free and see where the story leads you.

Below a group member wrote of her hopes for the future from the prompt, "Imagine you are alone on an island, and a bottle washes ashore with a message in it. What does it say?"

**ANOTHER VOICE**

### *Message in a Bottle* by Jo Bobbie

The bottle floated up to shore, and I eyed it suspiciously from the sand. But I got up and rescued it, feeling like I was doing someone a favor. I uncorked the top and shook the paper free. It was old and crinkled and was a letter saying that I would meet someone very nice for myself in the next six months, that I wouldn't be lonely any longer. Really? I thought. It also said this would be followed by good health and longevity.

I thought it was very nice that someone had written this wish for a total stranger, especially since I had been thinking for myself that my bipolar illness was a smaller monster in my mind lately. I was more confident and less worried about its return. Now I had been to the beach and touched on good fortune. A year ago I might not have been able to get to the beach at all. And so I took the message to heart. I left the bottle behind, wanting it to be an adventure for someone else. I looked out over the horizon, smiling, and decided to go for a long walk.

### *to write*

#### AN OLD, OLD LETTER

When you receive an unopened letter written to your great-great-grand-father, lost at the post office for one hundred years and now forwarded to you—what does it say? What do you do?

# *Where to Go Next*

This chapter has focused on fiction writing as it can be used in ways that are known to be healing, such as changing perspectives and creating happier endings, but of course there is much, much more to the world of writing fiction. The *Bibliography and Selected Resources* section includes suggestions of fiction-writing books to explore if you'd like to learn more.

Many people find that fiction is one of their favorite forms of writing once they use writing prompts to get over their initial uncertainty about it. As you develop a character and a situation into a full story, one where some dissatisfaction leads to some satisfaction and resolution, you may find that your unconscious mind offers you not just unique details and interesting plot twists, but brilliant metaphors, too. Write intuitively, carefully describe the images that come to you, feel the feelings that come up, and enjoy the surprises.

# Chapter 10

# *The Benefits of Sharing Your Writing*

*It is important to read aloud what you write. . . . It is part of the writing
process, like bending down to touch your toes and then standing
up again. . . . At first it is a very scary thing to do. . . .
But no one has ever died of it, so don't worry.*

—NATALIE GOLDBERG, *Wild Mind*

Now that you've begun to explore journaling, freewriting, poetry, memoir, and fiction as means of writing to ease depression, let's turn to the important, but lesser-known part of the writing-to-heal process: sharing your work with others.

Many well-known authors, including Virginia Woolf, have been vehement that a piece of writing is not finished until it is read by another. I have mixed feelings about this issue, since I believe that some very valuable writing is done for yourself—as presumably do millions of writers keeping private journals. However, it's undeniable that sharing what you've written adds an entirely different dimension to your writing experience.

Depression can be very lonely; we tend to isolate ourselves, and those around us don't always understand what we're going through. So sharing your writing is another aspect of the process that, while not required, often greatly enhances the healing experience. Among other benefits, disclosing your words is one means of reducing the loneliness by helping you forge powerful connections with other people.

Sharing what you've created is not always easy—in fact, the idea may sound frightening to you. We are all vulnerable when we open ourselves and our work to others, whether we are exploring our depression or any other topic. Professional writers and artists of all kinds must face these fears daily. For me, anxious though I may be at first, the result of handing a page of writing to a relative or reading a piece aloud to a depressed friend or group is usually more than worth the effort to open up. I've found numerous benefits from sharing my writing and from reading or listening to that of others. This is largely what led me to begin the writing group I've now led for ten years.

In this chapter, we'll look at some of the safe and rewarding ways you can communicate with peers and others who are close to you, such as family, friends, or your mental health care provider. Note that in chapter 11, we'll look at ways to share your writing with a broader audience, the public, by giving speeches and publishing your work. And then there will be much more discussion of how to find others to write with about depression, including developing a group, in chapter 13.

## Choosing Your Confidantes

Benefits, such as understanding and support, can come from depressed peers, from friends or family members, and from mental health care professionals. Each audience may elicit different feelings for you.

One way to develop powerful, caring alliances is to write with other depressed persons—in a partnership or writing group, either in person or online—and to read aloud or exchange your words. If you're communicating about your depression, it can be tremendously uplifting to discover other people who've "been there"—who comprehend your intense feelings about emotional upheaval, your fears of depression never leaving, your frustration at medicines and their side effects, or your sadness about the relationship or career damages you've sustained through this condition. Regardless of the topic you're exploring, you're growing as a writer too, and sharing these pieces can also be empowering and important.

Positive feedback on your writing, as well as understanding and support, can also come from others who haven't experienced depression—such as family, friends, a therapist, a doctor, or a general writing group—when you allow them to read your work or read aloud to them. By expressing your feelings, ideas, and experiences, you let them hear your voice as a writer, no matter your topic. If you share about your depression, you may be helping them comprehend for the first time who you are and what you're going through. At first, many writers with depression find sharing with this circle of people more difficult than sharing with depressed peers. But our confidence tends to increase with practice, just as our ability to write our truth increases with practice.

## Defining Your Feedback Rules

No matter who your audience is, it's crucial to lay down a few ground rules first if the sharing experience is to be a positive one. The most important of these is that you and your listener or reader agree that the material shared will be kept absolutely *confidential* unless you state otherwise. Second, there should be *no critiquing*, unless you specifically request feedback on your writing craft or advice on content.

Explain before you read that this is a personal piece of art you have chosen to share. Tell the listener or reader up front that it is fine for him or her to simply say, "Thank you for sharing that with me." If you wish to receive feedback, let the person know that it is all right to offer positive comments *on the writing*. For example, it might be gratifying to be told, "I was deeply touched by your description of depression"; it's *not* acceptable to be told, "I don't think that made much sense" or "You should really try this treatment my friend uses." If you do seek advice on the content of your writing, be sure to save that conversation until after any discussion of the writing itself or for another time.

> It's healing to be heard.
>
> —Jenny

Don't be thrown if there is a moment of quiet after you finish reading aloud. It often takes listeners a moment to absorb your words, especially when they are very moved by them. If a listener starts to give feedback when you've requested that he not, interrupt him, saying, "I'm not ready for any feedback on this right now." You need to receive encouragement on your fragile new piece of writing first, especially when you are new to reading aloud.

Be sure to keep these feedback rules in mind as you receive other writers' works as well. Honor others' writing; honor your own.

## Sharing with Others Who Experience Depression

Writing and reading with others who have depression can be very empowering. However, I've had many group members who were initially very uncomfortable with the idea of reading their works aloud and who always chose to "pass" when it was their turn. (You should never feel pressured to read aloud in a writing group for depression.) But in every case, they changed their minds within a meeting or two and began to read aloud. Often these are the very people who later tell me that reading, and listening to others read, is the most healing part of the group for them. So if you're hesitant to share your writing in such a situation, consider eventually pushing yourself a bit past your comfort zone and see what happens.

When you write a piece about depression—freewriting, poem, story, whatever—and plan to share it with other people with depression, you may begin to feel freer to dig into your emotions and the events that surround them. These are people who "get it." And as you offer up your words, you may find that you feel more accepted than you sometimes do just living with depression in everyday life. As you hear or read their writing, you are likely to identify with what they are saying. Then the circle goes round and round—you feel freer and more accepted as you write and share and then you deeply comprehend their experiences, which leads you to feel even more free and accepted as you do your next writing. What a powerful bond!

Another benefit of sharing writing back and forth with others coping with this condition is that you may find that you are helping another person too—and this wonderful feeling is very healing. Depression tends to draw our focus inward so much that there's often little energy left to help or heal others. Yet, by simply being an audience for another human's deep and perhaps painful feelings, you provide immense validation. This validation doesn't need to come from effusive compliments. Again, offering just brief positive comments—*without* giving advice or critiquing—or simply honoring the person's words with a quiet moment is best.

## Sharing with Loved Ones and Mental Health Care Professionals

If you choose to explore your thoughts and feelings about your depression by writing alone, without a partner or group, you can still consider sharing your work with family, friends, a therapist, or a doctor. This is somewhat different than sharing with a peer group because these people may never have experienced a serious depression. However, it can still be very beneficial. Even in these situations, the feedback rules should apply, at least initially: the writing is confidential, it is not to be critiqued, and no advice is to be given until or unless you say so.

Depression can be hard for family and friends to grasp sometimes. Through your writing, you might discover that you are teaching them about the pain of this condition in general and improving their understanding of your personal feelings and needs in particular. Sharing your writing with family or friends may open up further dialogue about the situation, including what events may have triggered the depression, which can be tremendously healing. Indeed, this eye-opening experience may even lead to specific offers of more support or necessary changes in your relationship. I wrote my mother a thank-you poem about how touched I was to receive flowers from her while on the psychiatric ward—a place where flower deliveries seem to be a rare occurrence—and together we were moved to instigate a whole new discussion about my hospital experience and what additional help I might need as I recovered.

Some writers choose to share their work with their therapist or psychiatrist. This can be a very rewarding way of opening up topics and emotions for further exploration in psychotherapy. It may be especially useful for introverts, who might initially feel safer writing than talking about the confusion and pain of their depression. I know people with depression who write before seeing a counselor, share those words during their session, and then write again after the meeting in order to capture their feelings about the latest discussion. In other cases, the therapist provides homework topics to write on. If this sounds appealing, you may want to suggest the idea to your therapist.

## Sharing Your Writing on Other Topics

Remember, the words you put down that aren't obviously related to your depression are very valuable, too. Whether you're writing on a past triumph, a strange dream, or a funny memory, it can be worthwhile to share it with others. In writing groups, I always try to offer an upbeat prompt for the last writing exercise of the day. This is especially important when we've entered deep emotions in the previous piece. Rather than dismissing these assignments as silly or superficial, most writers are eager to read their work on lighter subjects too, and we often share laughter from these pieces. Your audience will get to know many more facets of you when you share on such topics, including your roles, life experiences, memories, ideas, and dreams for the future. I find that this sort of sharing helps me define myself, feel a connection with others, and discover commonalities with others, and, if I request it, it provides feedback on how I might refine my work. All of these are healing to me.

*I find it is very helpful, and I feel better, when I read my words [aloud] and listen to what others are writing.*

—Diane

I've also been warmly touched to hear from one longtime member of our writing group for depression that whenever she visits her parents, the three of them sit around a table each morning, choose a topic, write together, and read aloud. They write on all sorts of subjects, and this process draws them closer. To me, this is a lovely illustration of how writing and communicating can be so powerful.

## Sharing Connects Us

Writing is itself a courageous act, and sharing your writing requires real bravery. You're exposing both the content of your words and the artistry with which you express them. It's important to start slowly and share first with people you consider very safe in order to reap its benefits.

Every human has a need to express him or herself in one way or another, but depression tends to turn this instinct down or off, and we tend to let our connections with the world wither away. Instead of always turning completely inward, we can use writing to reconnect and heal.

*to write*

### SHARING

Write about a time you shared something personal—perhaps a childhood story you told your children, a secret aspiration you shared with a friend, or maybe saying "I love you" to someone.

Then consider this: Was that experience a positive one? If not, are there ways, such as using guidelines, that might have improved it for you?

### THE MEANING OF A DREAM

Have you had a dream that left you musing about it later? Describe the dream, using all the sensory details you can—colors, noises, bodily sensations. As you write, ponder what, if any, meaning it might hold for you.

Then consider this: would you be comfortable reading this to another person? If so, experiment with a safe person, using the guidelines in this chapter. Then write about how it went.

In the piece below, a writing group member muses on a recurring dream. Writing about dreams is quite popular in the group.

### A Dream by Bill Scholtz

My favorite dream is one of flying. I used to have it often and hated to wake up. Perhaps I was a bird in a previous life. I hate airplanes—so cramped and noisy, they can't compare to levitating over the countryside in silent comfort.... Maybe it is a desire to rise above the mundane problems of being earthbound and realize that we are capable of much more joy and lightness than we are presently experiencing. Maybe the dream is just an expression of a deep desire to be free of gravity. Or perhaps [to be] like some reptiles who transcended crawling and walking and grew feathers and wings to become birds.

# Chapter 11

# *Writing for a Wider Audience: Publication and Speeches*

*I write for myself and strangers. This is the only way that I can do it.*

—GERTRUDE STEIN

Now you have begun to explore the world of writing, you've examined some of your inner world, including the lows of your depression; you've perhaps discovered whether you prefer freewriting to poetry or memoir to fiction; and you've discovered which of your stories you're most driven to communicate. You may have shared your words with others close to you, with depressed peers, or with mental health care professionals. The healing you've achieved may leave you feeling satisfied with your plan to continue your writing habit for yourself and those close to you—or you may feel a drive to step out into the world at large and tell your tales.

This chapter discusses making the choice to share your writing publicly. You might do this by publishing your work in periodicals or books or by speaking to groups. This decision may immediately sound exciting, even liberating, but it is not one to be taken lightly, especially when you consider unveiling your very personal stories about your depression. In addition, entering the huge field of writing professionally is like beginning any new career—it takes time, energy, a lot of learning, and probably some luck. However, if you sense that going public is a key part of your healing, you may find it tremendously gratifying.

# One Group's Experiences "Going Public"

Excitement ran high when my writing group began collecting contributions for its first anthology, which we titled *BrainStorms*. For most of the writers, this would be a first opportunity to see their work "in print," though instead of publishing it, we were creating a "chapbook"—binding our writing and artwork together into a booklet with a laminated cover and making numerous copies. The writing we gathered ran the emotional gamut from the description of a cherished doll to painful memories of rape and suicide attempts. It was important to its authors. Here they had complete pieces to show others as well as something tangible to look back on. It represented their emotional investment and hard work in the group, and it, like true publication, offered their honest feelings and thoughts to the world at large. They claimed their experiences by making others aware of them.

"Thanks for giving me an opportunity to have my writing in print. It was a funny (but good) feeling to see something so personal 'out there' like that," wrote Kim afterward. "Our book explores complicated issues and left me proud of our achievement. We've been able to put our thoughts into words and we're willing to share them with each other," Lindsey reflected. Other writers also reported sharing *BrainStorms* with people close to them, including their therapists and doctors, and felt validated by taking this step.

Several group members chose not to contribute any writing, even with the option that their names not be attached to the pieces. They were not pressured; their decision was honored immediately. Each person had individual reasons for not putting his or her words into the larger arena. Some didn't want it to affect their ongoing explorations with writing, others weren't comfortable with their artistry, or, most commonly, many simply preferred to keep their personal stories private. Just as no one should ever feel pressured into reading aloud in a writing group for depression, no one should be badgered to participate in a group publication project. Serious issues are involved in any writer's sharing of her work, and the emotional ramifications of making your depression public are especially significant.

# My Decision to "Go Public" with My Writing on Depression

I'm not exactly sure when I first began to share my own story publicly. But one early experience made a strong impression on me. I was taking part in a several-weeks-long creativity class that involved experimenting with a variety of media, including painting, collage, music, and writing. Near the end, we were invited to share some of our results with the rest of the class. I was depressed and feeling timid; I hesitated when my turn came. But glancing around the circle of faces I knew only slightly, I took a deep breath and began reading a poem I had written about my fear and confusion at having "heard voices" during my recent very serious mood swing.

It was scary to share this—would they write me off as a self-absorbed weakling or dismiss me as a "crazy" and therefore worthless person? When I tentatively looked up at the end, the woman across the room burst into tears. "You brought her back to me," she whispered with a small smile as she wiped her cheek. "My mother was schizophrenic and she died two years ago, and you brought her back to me. Now I know how she must have felt. Thank you, thank you for reading that."

Suddenly I felt the happiest I'd felt for weeks. My heart melted that evening, or perhaps my inhibitions about telling my truth melted. Despite all the stigma I feared I might encounter sharing my odd symptoms and my deep despair, and despite my concerns about the poetic merits of my nascent work, I realized I could profoundly touch someone with my writing. This, I instantly realized, meant that it was possible to make something meaningful out of my painful pointless depressions. The months, even years, of my life that I felt I was losing to the illness could have some redemption if I could use them to help another. I knew I would start sharing my words more widely.

Since that experience, I have found that owning my depression in articles, poetry, and speeches, and thereby claiming my place in the world, is freeing and uplifting. It validates for me that I have made progress with my recovery and that I belong to society just as much as a healthy person does (something I begin to doubt when I'm really down). Writing for the public about depression also helps me feel I'm doing something to help combat the still-pervasive societal stigma that surrounds all types of mental illness.

> *to write*
>
> ## MAKING YOUR WRITING PUBLIC
>
> **Freewrite about how it would feel to have the neighbors read your writing in a magazine or to have your parents hear you read your work aloud in an auditorium. Does it sound exhilarating—something you'd be very proud of? Does it sound like the last thing in the world you'd want to do? Whatever the case, also reflect in your writing on why you think you feel that way.**

## Some Reasons to Keep Your Writing Private

Many questions must accompany the decision of whether to expose your writing. Most important, you can't take back your words once you have offered them in public. You must assume that your acquaintances, your extended family, all your friends, your colleagues, and any future boss or date will know about your trials and your depression. It's amazing how one little article or a description of one short speech can get around, and fast, even when you don't want it to.

You need to consider that, because depression is still not well understood or accepted in our society, you may face criticism or condescension. For example, after giving many talks to groups about my experiences, I still feel a little hurt and angry when a person tells me I don't really need to take medicine if I just believe in God or I shouldn't have "allowed" myself to receive ECT.

You also need to weigh the fact that those close to you may be embarrassed by your depression. My family has been very supportive of me and this decision, but not everyone is so fortunate. Even more serious, you need to examine the situation if your story includes "outing" family members or others whose actions may have harmed you and led to your depression.

I highly recommend talking with your mental health professional about these issues before deciding whether you want to speak publicly or publish your writing. In addition, several of the books on writing memoir that are listed in the *Bibliography and Selected Resources* section may be helpful in their discussions of sharing your writing publicly, particularly when sticky family issues are involved.

## Start Learning about Publishing Your Writing

Like every writer, you'll need to edit, rewrite, and polish almost any piece you hope to publish in a magazine or newspaper, either traditional or online. Standards are high, and sloppiness of any kind will lead to a quick rejection slip. For this you need intelligent, knowledgeable feedback on your work, so I highly recommend that you join a writing group—one composed of writers working on a variety of subjects, not just depression. Look for notices in libraries, bookstores, and coffeehouses, and at writing classes or workshops, or post your own flier asking for other writers to join you on a regular basis to give encouragement and feedback on each other's work. As when you share writing with anyone, you'll need to set ground rules before the first person reads aloud so that people offer encouraging "positive" feedback as well as constructive "helpful" feedback. Attacking you or your work for any reason is not acceptable. Feedback from other serious writers will improve the way you tell your story, and as you listen and react to others, you also learn a tremendous amount. Several fine books describe working with other writers in detail, including *Writing Alone and with Others* by Pat Schneider (Oxford University Press, 2003) and *Writing Alone, Writing Together* by Judy Reeves (New World Library, 2002).

Read about writing and about how and where to submit your work. Look at *Poets and Writers* magazine and *Writer's Digest* as well as the books in the *Bibliography and Selected Resources* section. There are books about every form of writing and publishing. In addition, start trying to attend some writers' conferences, workshops, and classes that apply to the genre you want to explore—poetry, nonfiction articles, first-person essays, or fiction, for example. There are some good free or low-cost events in most areas. Search online and get yourself on the mailing lists of the writing groups near you. You can also look into adult education classes or community college classes to start. If you prefer, explore some of the many online writers' communities, where you can read, journal, get feedback on work, take classes, talk about writing, and more. Some of these are suggested in the *Bibliography and Selected Resources* section, too.

## Where Should You Try to Get Published?

The key strategy to use for getting published is to start with smaller-audience publications, either traditional or online, and work your way up to the big, very well-known ones. For writing on major depression or bipolar disorder, a good place to start is to submit your work to a mental health newsletter or to a mental health arts project. For example, many chapters of the National Alliance on Mental Illness and of the Depression and Bipolar Support Alliance publish periodicals regularly; your local clinic or hospital may also put out newsletters. The *Awakenings Review* is a literary journal that is written completely by people with mental illness. Local community newspapers also may publish articles on depression or be looking for local writers' first-person essays. These can be good ways to see how you feel about having your work in public.

If you succeed in smaller markets and you want to submit to magazines or newspapers with wider circulation, be sure to look at a current edition of *Writer's Market*, a thick book updated and published annually by Writer's Digest Books. It describes and lists contact information for thousands of publications. In most cases, as you approach larger publications you'll need to present copies of already published articles, known as *clips*, along with your carefully written *query letter* in order to prove you have published successfully before. If you are already thinking of writing and publishing a book, you'll almost certainly need clips to present with your formal book proposal to potential agents and editors. These suggestions are barely scratching the surface of a huge field. There is a lot more in the *Bibliography and Selected Resources* section about places to begin learning about how and where to publish.

Another great way to get your thoughts to the public is to develop a blog—which allows instant publishing online, but which lets you determine your audience through a variety of privacy options. A *blog* (short for "web log") is something like a newspaper column that you create and can add writing to at any time (for example, posting one of your new poems or essays or articles every few days). Anyone online can read your work (it generally shows up in search engines) and, if you choose, readers can make written comments back to you. I've had a blog for years, WriteOutOfDepression.blogspot.com, where I post writing exercises and articles I've written about mental health news and research, and I've developed a loyal readership.

You can also journal about mental health issues at various online sites (for example, HealthyPlace.com). Remember, however, that even if you delete something you've posted online with your name, it has still been made public and may be available through web archives.

A final, important thought about publishing in nearly any medium: you're bound to get some rejections, so be prepared. Competition is fierce. When one publication turns you down, learn from whatever comments you might get from that editor (if any; you'll often get only a form letter), and send your work out again to another publication. This happens to every writer, so don't be too discouraged. Selection criteria are very subjective, and good material often gets overlooked and later published elsewhere. Definitely don't allow a rejection of one piece by one person to change your conviction that you are a valid writer with a unique and important voice, that you began writing because you felt it eased your depression, and that it still holds that magical ability.

## To Speak or Not to Speak Your Words?

When I began writing up my thoughts and speaking publicly about my struggles with bipolar depression, I was anxious. My mood disorders support group at the time had elected me to be on a panel speaking to a community organization about depression. But I recalled my feelings of triumph after reading my poem in the creativity class and found that after sharing my written words with this larger, completely unknown audience, my spirit was fortified once again.

People listened intently as, page by page, I unwound my story of becoming ill, the dozens of treatments, the ups and downs over the years, the progress I'd made, and my dreams for the future—all created by editing several freewritings on these topics. Afterward, when audience members approached me, was the most gratifying time of all. Some shyly admitted they had experienced depression and embraced me, saying that my words rang true for them and left them feeling less isolated; others said they now understood their depressed relatives better. I can scarcely think of anything more rewarding. And it felt thrilling to consider that perhaps I had made a difference in the lives of those I spoke to.

Over the years, I've now spoken about mental health and my story to many groups, on behalf of a number of organizations. My audiences have included police officers, physicians and medical students, substance abuse clients and staff, mental health workers, depressed persons and their families, church groups, and a variety of community groups. Although I now generally speak without notes, my carefully prepared words were initially key to building my confidence. Like writing for publication, writing your own speeches and presenting them publicly is not to be taken lightly. Talk about the decision first with your mental health care professional and consider how this may affect your life and those of others.

Two national organizations that offer speakers' programs, including training you to tell your story and arranging speaking engagements, are the National Alliance on Mental Illness and the Depression and Bipolar Support Alliance. You may also want to explore local mental health groups, such as your county mental health association, hospital, or clinic, or local psychology classes or crisis centers. Such organizations are often glad to have speakers offer their services, and they provide good venues in which to present your words and story.

## It's Up to You

Since we are always refining our own life stories in our minds, telling our tales can be personally validating. And, as I've described, it can feel very rewarding to raise awareness of mental health issues. Often by telling our own stories, we offer the most meaningful examples of how people coping with depression or other conditions can recover and function in society, and how we should be respected, not stigmatized. But speaking out, telling your own truth to the world, and writing for a larger audience are difficult tasks, and they must be undertaken at the proper time for *you*.

I remember when, back in graduate school, I talked to the one fellow student with whom I had shared much of my depression situation, telling him that I had vague fantasies about writing a book on this strange state. He immediately recommended writing my story as fiction in order to avoid the prejudice and professional discrimination that I might trigger with a personal memoir. For me, at that time, he was probably right. It was several years before I began sharing my experiences with depression through my poetry, speeches, and articles. And by then, for me, that was the right decision, too. Start with small steps if you feel compelled to write for a wider audience, and take your time learning whether this is a healing activity for you.

*to write*

## WHAT DO YOU WANT TO SAY?

Imagine you have fifteen minutes to speak to a club of businesspeople about depression, and freewrite about what you would like to say. Is your message that people can overcome depression? Does it concern the quality of mental health care in our society? Do you want to show how stigma can harm depressed people so that they fail to seek treatment? Is it a plea for research money for a particular project? And how can you use your personal story to illustrate your points?

# Chapter 12

# *Writing with Your Depression, Not against It*

> *In a way I used up some of my loneliness by writing.*
>
> —TRUMAN CAPOTE, IN *Writers on Writing*

Depression hurts. There's no way around it. If you've felt the ache of sadness that comes from who knows where, the weighted limbs, the lethargy that means you spend all day thinking about showering but not doing it, you know. Now that you've been doing exercises and you've learned about several writing genres and techniques to use as you develop a writing habit and even consider sharing, you may feel fired up and ready to crank out words on the page—or you may feel you're unable to get started.

If it's the latter, this chapter is here to help. Here you'll find more suggestions and techniques, hints, and ideas about ways to get moving and keep moving—and become a better writer in the process. If you're eager to give writing a try as one of your depression treatments but feel stuck, this may just trigger you to open that new notebook you bought with good intentions but haven't touched yet. Be open. Be curious. And stretch yourself to check out these tips and find what works well for you.

## *You're Not Alone*

First, remember, you *can* do this, even when you're down. Others have done this before you. Many, many writers through the ages have managed to create while depressed and found that it was healing to push themselves.

Author John Nichols, as quoted in *The Vein of Gold* by Julia Cameron (Tarcher/Putnam, 1996), said: "One thing I learned real early in my career is that if you wait for the perfect mood, or the perfect place, or the perfect situation for writing, you'll never write a word. . . . And you have to write if you're miserable. If you're uninspired. If you're sick. If you're totally depressed. . . . [T]here's never a perfect time for writing. Even the concept is absurd."[1]

So take courage, and keep reading and writing.

## I Don't Know What to Write About!

So many beginning writers complain that they have nothing to write about. This is never true—everyone has experienced love or a loss, thirst, or a lavender sunset. You in particular, as a person grappling with depression, have a huge amount of material available to you, even if you've never climbed Mount Everest. You've experienced a profound inner state and you have a lot to say. You have something unique to draw upon creatively.

There's a famous old writing adage that says: *write what you know.* To begin, try focusing on what you yourself have actually experienced when you develop topics, emotions, and thoughts in your writing. Use that experience. That is the place to start. In addition, your writing will be much more alive and believable if it is grounded in your own world—including your very important experiences with depression.

When you're sitting down to write, feeling depressed and crummy, start with what you know at that moment—your own thoughts about how you hate how often you're watching soap operas and how you really are lazy and there are still dirty dishes from yesterday, there's no gas in the car, your spouse didn't mow the lawn, and what in the world is there for dinner? And start with your feelings right now, too—sad that your child left for college, dread over that party invitation for Friday, hopeless because you can't remember what day it is, fear over next week's job interview. Pour those ruminations onto the page—this is the introspective journaling approach.

I always feel clearer and lighter after doing this. Often I start with this in-the-moment check-in with myself even if I'm sitting down to work on another piece of writing, just to clear the fog from the top of my mind so I can move on to other ideas. Writing what you know, including your depression, provides a foundation for your other writing. After this warm-up, switch gears and try freewriting on a specific topic. Try something related, if you want to explore your depression from a new angle, or try something completely different—last time you had a belly laugh, a time you danced, apples, the color yellow. Remember to write continuously for the whole time you've set for yourself.

## *to write*

### A FAMILY MEMBER WITH DEPRESSION

**Do you have a family member—or a friend or an acquaintance—who has experienced a significant depression or another mood disorder or perhaps anxiety? Describe that person, how he or she coped with the condition, and whether that holds any meaning for you.**

Reflecting upon a family member who had a mental illness helped this group member find context for her own bipolar disorder.

### ANOTHER VOICE

*Auntie Fann* by Katherine Lerer

The only glimpse of mental illness that probably was present in retrospect in my family was my father's sister, my Auntie Fann. She would sit at our large dining room table, often with eight or nine people around it, and sigh heavily over her food in a hunched position. She had had a rather tragic life. She had a brief marriage of two years before her husband learned the combination to the safe at our family's scrap iron and metal dealership in San Francisco. He ran away with the money. She was about twenty-five. She never recovered from the humiliation and shock, and she lived almost all of her life with her parents.

After her mother's death (our grandmother), Auntie Fann, with her sighing, slumping, and bleak behavior, moved into our home for about ten years. Later, at about fifty-five, she moved to an apartment with an attendant. She died three years later of complications due to diabetes. In retrospect, I honestly don't know if she died by suicide.

I cringe now as I look back at how unsympathetic and unloving I was to her as a young girl. I ignored her and didn't often kiss her. I just went about my business and sometimes teased her along with my brothers and sister. But there were times when we were kind and she was too. She took us down to Market Street with its hubbub of movie theaters. We would see films with her after going to the special popcorn store next door to get caramel corn or popcorn with lots of butter. She would wear her fox stole; you could push a lever near the mouth of the fox to hook it securely around your neck.

I also remember how she used to moan and become frightened very easily, particularly during the earthquakes we would have in San Francisco. I picture her in our downstairs den, where we had the television set, sitting comfortably in a tall brown leather armchair, when the earth began to shake. Her words were, "Oh my god. Oh my god. Momma. Momma." The four of us children were more relaxed than she was, reassuring her that it was going to be all right.

Auntie Fann also played the piano in the living room, and the furniture and antiques she purchased for our home were ones that my mother kept until her own death. Auntie Fann knew good quality and vintage pieces. I have her jewelry, and I can remember so vividly her wearing the black onyx pieces. When I wear one of them when I feel ill, I always rub it and use it as a talisman.

Auntie Fann, I'm so sorry I didn't know the torment you felt all those years. How brave and how kind you were to us. It's remarkable you stayed alive as long as you did, because I wouldn't have. Today I admire you enormously. You ended up being a role model.

## *Mental Jump Starts*

The following suggestions may get you writing when you feel sluggish or sad and it seems your brain isn't quite working right. Try them out and see which become your favorites.

- Keep a page in your notebook where you **jot down any ideas** of things you'd like to write about. Later, if you feel depressed and unfocused when you sit down to write, turn to your list for ideas.

- I'm a big fan of using lists in other ways, too. If you want to write about a big abstract subject like freedom, destiny, friendship, or depression, start by **brainstorming a very quick list** of related topics or examples. Don't evaluate these items; just put them down. After three or four minutes, or when you've gotten down everything you can think of, choose one item and start with it. Keep to a single illustrative example before jumping to sweeping generalizations. You'll feel more satisfied when you can get your mind around the topic by using specifics, and your writing will be clearer, too.

- If you're a visual thinker, try "**clustering**" to bump your mind into gear by making connections among ideas. On the center of a clean sheet of paper, write a word or short phrase you'd like to explore in your writing ("coffee," for example) and circle it. Then draw several lines radiating out from the circle like sunbeams. At the end of each line, write a related word or phrase ("coffee cup," "caffeine," "coffeehouse," "breakfast," "espresso") and circle it so it looks like lollipops are coming out of the center circle. Add as many lines and circles as you need. Then brainstorm to make a third level of ideas by sending out at least one other line from the head of each lollipop and placing new words or examples there (from "caffeine," I put "energy," "shaky," "insomnia"). Circle these ideas and continue as needed. Use this technique to break down and organize a topic that feels overwhelming, or simply to generate ideas. For example, see what you come up with starting from just a word about what's in front of you right now, whether it's a blue jay or a photo of your nephew.

- Move your writing to the next level. Start by journaling about your thoughts and feelings in the present moment. After describing your current state for ten minutes or so, reread what you've just written and **circle a few words** or ideas that strike you as the most exciting or interesting or curious. Then immediately begin writing again using one of those as your starting point. You may find that this second writing is more rewarding because it focuses on what you truly wanted to write about but didn't realize before—or because it takes you away to the story about the medieval princess you've been wanting to get around to. Don't control your writing too much; just let go and let yourself be surprised.

- **Try writing a letter**. (You'll decide later whether to send it, crumple it, or burn it; for now, just write it.) Consider describing how your depression really feels to a relative or an old friend who doesn't "get it." Or write a letter to a deceased relative whom you remember fondly. Write to a loved one about what you need most from her right now. Write to your therapist or doctor about what has most helped you lately or what you're currently concerned about, especially if you find writing about sensitive topics easier than talking about them. Draft a letter to yourself describing your great qualities, which you may have neglected to notice lately. Or try a completely different topic—tell a friend about your pet's latest antic or your favorite movie of all times.

- **Write from other mental states you already know well**. If you know how to focus and cram for an exam, use that intensity, even for a short writing session, to push yourself into a different mental zone. Do you like to be outdoors? Take your notebook on a long walk and write immediately after enjoying the wildflowers or rock formations to see how that contentment affects your ideas and words. Do you meditate? Close your eyes and capture that state of awareness of your mind and breath, and then, maintaining that mindfulness, begin writing.

- **Writing is physical**—use that motion of your typing fingers or moving hand and be aware of it in your whole body—let your writing flow with it. If you've ever gotten involved in playing a sport or dancing so that you lost track of time, try to recapture that nonthinking state in your body as you push the pen across the page.

- **Read**, even a little, if your depression possibly allows you to. Read anything you love before you begin a writing session, whether it's Dostoyevsky or *Sports Illustrated*. Then, without thinking or getting up, begin to write. You might write in response to what you read or you can try writing on another topic in that writer's style or "voice." Or let a word or an idea you read send you down a completely new path.

- Do you really feel you can't read due to your depression? Take a favorite book, or any book, open it randomly, and **put your finger down somewhere on the page**. Take the word under your fingertip and use it as a writing prompt.

- Finally, keep in mind that you do not need to focus your writing solely on depression and its related issues. Try **alternating more positive topics with the very difficult ones**. For example, write on something you never thought about before by grabbing one of the prompts in chapter 14 or from one of the other books listed in the *Bibliography and Selected Resources* section. And consider making it a habit to end a writing session on a good note—we do this regularly in my writing group. If you're near the end of a disturbing writing session, at least take time to write down three things you are grateful for. It does make a difference.

*to write*

### LIST MAKING

Quickly make a list of at least twenty-five things you're good at. They might range from kissing to remembering to send birthday cards to fixing a flat tire to reading a map to balancing a checkbook to doing rocket science. Then choose one, large or small, and write for twenty minutes on that skill. Who taught it to you? What's the secret to it? Do you love doing it? How could someone else learn it?

# Heal—and Become a Better Writer

Great empowerment and healing can come from rendering a story—a tale with a setting, a problem that occurs, and a resolution—in a way a reader or listener can really grasp and understand. This is how we best process the events of our lives, and this also tends to make for the best writing. Now, starting by writing what you know, try applying three new guidelines: Show, don't tell. Be specific. Use your senses.

*Show, don't tell*, is another well-known writing maxim. It means that by letting the reader experience what's happening in a piece of writing, you'll engage her much more than if you simply state what occurred.

Which is more compelling? "She was tired as she entered the kitchen and smelled the dinner cooking" or "The old woman shuffled across the checkered linoleum, eased herself into a wooden chair at the scratched round table, then lifted her head, sniffed, and looked toward the simmering pot on the stove with a small smile."

Now, instead of merely telling your notebook, "I was so depressed this morning," you can show it: "I cried for two hours on the sofa after breakfast and hid in the bathroom instead of answering the doorbell when it rang." This is much more powerful, and the reader gets the message even more clearly.

Another important guideline emphasized by many teachers is: *be specific*. Writing, for example, that "The woman signed the letter" is not nearly as interesting or informative as, "The white-haired matron quickly autographed the carefully lettered scroll with her black fountain pen."

When writing about your depression, you can use specifics to name and deeply explain how you feel. This in itself may help you feel less overwhelmed by these emotions and certainly describes your condition better to your friend, doctor, or therapist, if you decide to share it. In this case, "I was sad and tired" might become, "I tried to smile, but my face muscles wouldn't. My throat was tight. My chest felt like it held a lead weight, and if I had put my head down on the table, I would have slept immediately."

Another key to writing is: *use your senses.* Use information from all of your five senses—or six, if you're so inclined—when you describe any scene. "He ate his lunch and looked out at the mountain" might become, "Earl, staring through the streaked glass at the spiked, snowy peaks, heard only the chickadees. As he lifted a spoon to his rough lips, the aroma of potatoes, cream, and butter reached his nose, priming his taste buds for the hot, savory soup." That's quite a difference.

Now think about how you can incorporate sight, sound, touch, taste, and smell into your writing, even about depression. "I couldn't sleep all night" could become much more meaningful by using even a few sensory details, for example, "I curled up under the warm, frayed patchwork quilt and counted the stripes in the wallpaper over and over until the window grew light yellow and the odor of aftershave wafted in from the adjoining bath, where Bob's off-key whistling was as loud as ever."

## to write

### A PROUD MOMENT

**Write about an event that made you feel proud. Describe what happened and how you felt by showing (not telling), using specifics, and using your senses. Let yourself delve into the details as if you are telling this fascinating story to a friend who's hanging on every word.**

## Facing Down Depression's Symptoms

I discussed previously the importance of developing a disciplined writing habit, but you also need to be kind to yourself about this—not lackadaisical, but kind. Here's the approach that I've found over the years works best for me: If you're in the midst of a depressive period, write when you can. Try hard to write something every day on your project. If you're working on a long project and even a small section is too overwhelming because of your mental health, just freewrite or journal for a few pages to keep your writing mind active. If even this is too much, then let it go for the day. Don't punish yourself or make yourself feel guilty. Just make a conscious decision to skip it today but to try again tomorrow. Remember, your health must come first,

*[T]he ongoing discipline of writing may help us ward off the most crippling aspects of depression.*

—Louise DeSalvo,
*Writing as a Way of Healing*

so don't allow a writing project to harm your health in any way. Kindly but firmly ask yourself to write each day. And remember that just getting over the hump of starting may in fact enhance your health considerably by providing catharsis, a distraction, and a sense of accomplishment.

My poor recall is another difficulty I face when writing pieces about the past, including my memoir. Memory can be adversely affected by depression itself and by some of the medications used to treat it. Also, my many treatments with ECT, which is notorious for causing short-term and sometimes extensive, long-term amnesia, left many "chunks" of my memory gone or extremely hazy. When I have had memory difficulties during my writing, I've discovered several things that help. First, writing about the bits of an event or a relationship I do remember often triggers more details, even when just thinking about it has left me blank. Failing that, I sometimes turn to someone who was with me during that time—my husband, mother, psychiatrist—and ask for his or her memories of it. This often triggers better recall for me. Then, if there were photos documenting these old situations, or old journal entries even hinting at them, I study these artifacts. Sometimes seeing an image from a particular era or details written in my own hand touches my mind in the mysterious way a dream does.

## Depression May Help Your Writing

Though you may sometimes find it difficult to fight your way through your depression to write, be aware that some writers and artists actually find it easier in this state. We recently discussed this in my writing group, and a handful of writers said they feel that they write more deeply and with better flow when depressed. When they were well, they found their writing lacked some depth. One writer, who is also a visual artist, believes that her paintings are more expressive when she is depressed. So be open and observe your own tendencies and habits, and determine how you personally can best write to ease your depression.

# III.

# WHERE TO GO FROM HERE

# Chapter 13

# *Writing and Healing in a Community of Peers*

*I think all artists, and especially poets, are forever in search of
a community. It's a solitary act, and you need a community of like-minded
souls to survive and to flourish.*

—STANLEY KUNITZ, U.S. POET LAUREATE, 2000

As you've learned, a writing group for people with depression is *not* group therapy. It is also not a typical critique group, where writers share their works in progress in order to receive feedback to better their craft. So what is the nature of this group of people who have depression and gather regularly to write? And what about it enhances the process of easing depression?

One important part of the answer is "peers"—other people who have also felt deep depression. My group members and I have found that, for us, the healing environment of peers enhances the writing process. In our group, a distressing common experience draws together strangers who join to create a true community—a place where writers who all know the pain of depression give voice to their deep thoughts, feelings, and stories; where each person is honored and validated; where people empower those around them; and where self-esteem and insight have opportunities to grow.

This chapter unveils the synergistic healing that writing in a group to ease depression can bring. First, it shows you more about how my writing group at Stanford operates, including some of the pain and the joy that can surface there. Second, we look at how a peer writing group for depression differs from a general writing critique group and how its benefits compare to those of general peer *support groups* for depression. Finally, this chapter will guide you if you are interested in developing your own writing group for people with depression, either online or in person.

* * * *

I've drifted completely away from my own writing as I ponder the histories of members of my writing group, who are freewriting about their childhood bedrooms. As my eyes travel around the table, they fall on Tom, who found one of the purple fliers I placed in the clinic and called me yesterday.

"Do I need to be a good writer?" he had asked tentatively.

"Absolutely no experience required," I reassured him.

"And do I have to read my writing to other people?"

"No," I answered this question, common among newcomers, "you can always choose to simply pass when we read aloud."

Ten years ago, as I worked my way, day by day, sometimes moment by moment, through the worst of my bleak depressions, I began to wonder whether a group like this was possible. As one medicine after another failed to help me, I took comfort in filling notebooks with my muddled thoughts, which very slowly coalesced into stories, poems, and bits of memoir. Gradually I began to gain some insight into the twists my life had taken. It dawned on me that writing might also provide a potent tool for others who were struggling to manage, and ultimately escape from, this beast of depression. Now scores and scores of writers have taken part in this group, privileging me with the opportunity to hear the stories and ideas they share. I love to have new members join in, but even more gratifying is watching veterans leave to take on volunteer positions, family responsibilities, even newly won jobs, as their health improves.

*There is no doubt in my mind that being in your writing class has been one of—if not the—most significant parts of my recovery.*

—HILLARY

"Okay, take about a minute to wrap up," I announce as I tear myself from my musings. As pens are set on the table and before I can say another word, Tom speaks up, a slightly perplexed look on his face. "So why are we writing about this—I mean, bedrooms instead of depression?" I have heard this type of query often from new students.

"Several reasons," I reply. "We often explore our mental health issues through writing and sharing here, but we write on other topics as well. Typically we'll start with some concrete prompt rather than an abstract idea. So an exercise like this helps us stretch our minds and awaken the creative parts of our brain as we begin an afternoon's session.

"Also, we sometimes write in crazy directions in this class just to see where our minds take us," I add. "But as you gain experience, you'll find that a topic like this can sometimes lead you to profound places—to memories and feelings you may not have touched for a while, even to connections you haven't made before. It can be very healing to organize and release those discoveries."

"*And*," says Leslie, jumping in, "reading your writing aloud on this kind of topic will get you used to us—although you'll find this is a very safe place."

I nod and then continue. "Another reason we might write about the beach or your favorite flower or a photo of a tiger is that different topics can make us stronger, better writers for writing on any topic, including depression. For example, some of the techniques we talk about from time to time in here are structuring our stories, using our senses, and describing details. These three things are among those that many authors, of both fiction and nonfiction, emphasize when teaching others how to hone their writing craft.

*I get to say my innermost thoughts and feelings out loud. I see others depressed who are beautiful spirits, so I must be a beautiful spirit too.*

—MAUDE

Also, these skills help us to better develop a narrative and to explore changes in perspective. Both those things have been found in studies to be likely to improve your health when you're writing directly about emotional or traumatic experiences—something we're more likely to address in the second exercise of the class."

# Reading Aloud

After a quick round of introductions to allow the group to meet Tom, and let Tom begin to learn members' names, we begin the ritual of reading our pieces aloud, working our way around the table. As people read, they settle into the feeling of transforming their written words into sounds to share with others. For new class members, this can be an unusual, even very frightening feeling, but with practice it becomes more comfortable. Eventually, many find reading aloud valuable and even enjoyable. We keep comments to a minimum for this round but listen carefully to each other.

In addition to descriptions of shag carpets, ruffled curtains, and looping train sets, we learn of a beloved twin sister who occupied the top bunk, the calico cat who always wanted the pillow for herself, and three young boys who escaped their summer boredom through an open window while parents slept.

Then Karen reads her account of a molesting big brother who stole into her room in the night when she was a child. Anything is fair game for those willing to unearth it and present it to this group.

"That's an incredibly powerful piece, Karen. I appreciate you trusting us and sharing it with us," I say softly, passing a box of tissues as I see a tear roll down her face.

Beside her, Renata squeezes her hand. "That happened to me when I was a kid, too. It's still very, very painful."

Karen whispers, "Thanks. I'm working on it in therapy," then takes a deep breath and turns to the next reader, indicating she is ready to move on.

It's not always obvious which prompts will lead to exploration of very serious topics. Students in this class have written on abuse, rape, broken promises and relationships, addictions, psychosis, losing loved ones, other serious illnesses, war experiences, suicide attempts, and more. Writing, I often emphasize to the group, can take us in surprising directions sometimes.

"You should always feel safe sharing here," I remind Tom and the rest. "No one will critique your writing unless you ask them to. And it's important for everyone to always remember that we have a confidentiality rule in this group: anything that is said here remains private and is not to be discussed outside of the group," I emphasize, referring to the agreement that each person signs when he or she joins the group. I know of only one time this contract was breeched, and some private material was unintentionally revealed; the act was frustrating for the woman whose material was shared, but after discussing it, she forgave the transgression.

*Fear of my disease had kept me isolated in a kaleidoscope of pain and memories. . . . [I]t is my peers who hold me steady, give me sunshine on my darkest days, and love me when I cannot love myself.*

—ROSE

We continue to listen to childhood recollections, and various readings are met with smiles, sympathetic looks, nods of familiarity or sadness, or loud laughter. Our emotions move quickly at times, but I work to assure each reader by making eye contact, perhaps giving a brief reflection of what I've heard, and offering a "Thank you" after he or she has spoken. The attentiveness of these peers—diverse in age and background but similar in their depression experiences and their desire to explore together—is what builds the bonds of trust that develop here.

## to write

### CAKE

**Sometimes seemingly simple prompts can lead us in surprising directions and into very meaningful material. Freewrite on the topic "cake." You might be led to your favorite recipe, a birthday party incident, your wedding, or somewhere else entirely. Be open to where the writing takes you.**

In this exercise, the simple warm-up topic "cake" led this group member to describe a beloved figure in her life and even to make spiritual observations.

### *Cake* by Heather Tolles

Yay!

Birthdays. Celebrations. Decadence. Borderline hedonism, by Heather standards! All that milk, white flour, and sugar—so bad, but so, so good! I had a fabulous rose cheesecake just last night—and maybe it was all the love and spiritual energy that went into it, but I think it was one of the best cakes I've ever eaten. For Asha's birthday. Her sixtieth, and she doesn't look a day over forty. You'd think that being a minister, foreswearing much of what most of us think of as pleasures, and assuming responsibility for the spiritual emergence and development of hundreds of people would age a person—but the opposite is obviously true. She is radiant. Absolutely beautiful, vibrant and energetic, joyful and peaceful, all to a degree [that] most people do not dream of attaining—in fact, most would do well to attain half of any one of these qualities in the abundance that Asha enjoys them.

Being near her is like eating a piece of that cake. A sweetness, a richness—a bliss I wish I could enjoy forever. Of course, for me, like most of us, that feeling is transient; it lasts only as long as I have another bite in my mouth, as long as I am in the presence of someone as radiant as Asha. But actually, that's the whole point of the spiritual path: learning to bake my own cake, so I can enjoy it whenever I have a craving.

# *Exploring Our Mental Health*

We move into the next part of the group. Each week I offer an optional homework assignment, which I also post on my blog, WriteOutOfDepression. blogspot.com. These ideas and suggestions are designed as prompts for individual writing during the week, which helps some students and other online readers maintain their regular writing practice. Now we listen as students read their homework as well as short stories and freewritings they have brought to share.

After taking time for brief announcements—in this case, I'm notifying members of a new contest I read about for writing on chronic health conditions—it's time to transition to an exploration exercise. Generally, this is a more serious prompt dealing with emotions, past experiences, or future plans. In some cases, these subjects deal directly with the writer's depression; at other times, they are more open-ended and each person can decide how deeply to dig.

"Write a letter to someone—alive or dead or imaginary—describing a difficulty your depression has caused and how you've coped with that," I announce. "Let's write for twenty minutes on this one. And remember, you're always free to write on another topic of your choosing, or to let your writing move to another subject as you put it down. Sometimes we really need to write on a particular topic at a particular time. And if the suggested topic sounds like an uncomfortable one to you today, try writing a letter checking in about what you've been doing this week instead."

*[Writing] validates my experience. I get emotional release from writing down what's in my head, discovering my own voice and story.*

*—Harriet*

This type of exercise usually calls for a longer period of time because it may lead to a lot of material for each person, and we all need a chance to emotionally process as we write. If the prompt specifically calls for an exploration of depression or another difficult emotion, I also offer an alternate topic for anyone who prefers it.

Twenty minutes later, we draw our writing to a close and begin to listen to each other read. I try to provide positive feedback for each reader, and the other listeners join in as well, praising a description or turn of phrase, sometimes asking for a repeat reading of a favorite line.

As usual, our creations vary tremendously. Allison reads a letter to her late mother about how her depression in the last year has left her unable to volunteer regularly at her son's school but how she hopes to help at a fund-raiser there next week. Celine's letter to an imaginary friend tells of her sadness over being fired from her high-tech sales career; she has written an encouraging letter back to herself from the imaginary friend as well. Jacob reads his letter to his father about his difficult decision to try life again after a suicide attempt and how he is now going forward with a psychotherapist.

Although these are difficult remembrances, this topic also invites writers to place these events in a perspective that may be new and positive by asking them to examine their coping strategies as well.

*to write*

## THE DEATH OF SOMEONE CLOSE

By the time we're adults, most of us have experienced the passing of someone dear to us, whether relative, friend, or pet. Describe the thoughts and feelings you had at a time of loss.

Then consider, in writing, how the death may have changed you as a person. Do you view the world any differently now?

In another exploration exercise, this group member recounted the story of her mother's death and her own part in easing her mother's passing.

### ANOTHER VOICE

*The Death of a Loved One* by Carolyn Turnbull

Mom was ninety-eight when she died three years ago in a nursing home in Nebraska. She'd been lucid up until a few months before when she'd slipped and fallen, hitting her head hard. My sister called all of us to let us know Mom was no longer herself—she was anxious, angry, crying repeatedly, "Help me, help me," although it was a childlike "Hep me," not a pronunciation she'd ever used. She clutched at whoever was near, and the only way to break the pattern was to hold her and say, right next to her ear, "It's okay. I'm here. I'll help you." She could be distracted with a drink of water or food but would return to pleading within minutes.

When I had visited last, I could still get through to her every once in a while with "Mom, I love you so much" or "You were the best mom" or "I've missed you so." She deserved all the loving things I could say to her, although at one point in my life, when I was struggling to get her to see me for who I was, not who she wanted me to be, I thought I hated her.

When my sister called me the last time to say Mom was dying, I booked a flight from San Francisco right away. As I drove to the airport, though, I wondered why I was rushing to fly back. If she was so incapacitated and inconsolable, how could I help? What good would it do to be there?

After the family had celebrated her ninetieth birthday, she'd told me that she was ready to die, that she was frustrated and waiting impatiently. Eight years later, it was finally time. She clutched and begged for help. I had asked my doctor what I could do, and she said, "Help her take leave. Tell her not to worry, that you and all your brothers and sisters are fine, and you'll all take care of each other. Tell her she can let go now."

Holding her hands, I told her this when she and I were alone in her room and she seemed to be asleep. The first time, afraid the nursing aids would hear me, I said it under my breath. The next day I tried again, speaking quietly aloud. I added that she could finally go to see my father, who had died twenty years earlier; my sister, who had died ten years before that; and her favorite sister, who had died a few years [before] at ninety. I even dared to include my youngest brother, who had died only a month [before] in Louisiana, although the family had agreed not to tell her about this because it would hurt her so badly. Her eyes were closed when I told her, and she didn't respond, as far as I could tell.

I stayed overnight with her. The next morning brought two of her granddaughters, only a few years younger than I, and over the course of a few hours as we chatted, catching up, she began to breathe more and more shallowly. . . .

Then . . . she stopped.

## Resolving Feelings

We typically have time for one more freewriting exercise during the two-hour group meeting when we have ten to fourteen people. (With fewer participants, there may be time for more.) I consider this third one a reflection exercise. It is intended to be thought provoking and also to help writers bring their focus and mood back from the emotional state they might be in from the previous writing. This enables us all to balance those challenging feelings with positive ones and to end the session in a comfortable state.

"Let's finish today with the following question," I suggest after our short discussion about the previous topic. "What would you like to tell the next generation?"

We write for ten minutes this time. I note that even faces that had looked sad or resigned before are relaxing now as writers focus on their pages. Pens move quickly.

When we read, there is greater diversity in the responses than I had imagined, yet certain themes are repeated. One writer apologizes for global warming, another for the current wars in the world; both offer ideas for resolving these problems. The next person addresses her grand-daughter directly with family history and reassur-ances for a good life ahead. One person explains his conclusions from years of spiritual searching. Several reach back to their own personal struggles and triumphs to direct future readers to "Be true to yourself," "Find what you love and follow it," and "Leave the world a little better than you found it."

*I don't feel alive unless I am writing about my experiences in the world. The more I can write, the better, whatever the topic.*

—JOHANNA

"Amen!" Kent declares loudly after the last reader finishes, and smiles go around the table. "That next generation is going to be very wise," he says.

## to write

### A MYSTERIOUS HAPPENING

Here's a simple question that may or may not have a simple response: what's the most mysterious thing that has ever happened to you?

In this reflection exercise, Lauren wrote a fascinating story on a strange occurrence.

## The Most Mysterious Thing That Ever Happened to Me
by Lauren Herzog Schwartz

My mother was an immigrant; she left Czechoslovakia right after the Nazis took over. Her parents had to prove to those in power that she had no money, property, or valuable assets before she was able to leave. She was nineteen when she arrived in the United States, all alone, knowing no one, speaking very little English. She attended university here and tried to become "American" as quickly as possible. By distracting herself she didn't have to think about what was going on with her family in Europe. Eventually, though, she was made aware that her parents and many other family members had perished in the concentration camps. She remained very busy and never allowed herself the chance to mourn. When she graduated, she moved to the big city and met my father.

It was very sad for me to grow up without grandparents. Everyone I knew had extended family, and all we had was each other. Because of the pain it caused her, my mother refused to talk about her prior life in Europe. As a young person, I never saw any photographs of her family.

As an adult, I moved across the country to begin a new life in California. There were times that I felt like a refugee, just like my mother. I began to immerse myself [in] drawing and painting for the first time. I surprised myself as I realized they had become a major part of my life. They were like oxygen to me. I couldn't breathe without them. At times I wouldn't know what I was thinking or feeling until I began making marks on paper.

Then I decided to try working with clay. I liked the feel of the cold, mushy dirt in my hands, and the wonderful earthly smell. Working with the clay came very naturally to me. It felt healing to work with. It was like giving myself a massage. One time I started working on a piece and had no idea where I was going with it. As I worked with it, the clay molded itself into a face—a man's face. He had deep sunken eyes and a large forehead. His lips were thick and formed into a sort of half smile. He began to seem like a real person. All of a sudden I knew that the clay had turned into the face of my grandfather, my mother's father who had died in the Holocaust.

Years later when I finally saw a photograph of him, I was astonished at the resemblance. Through the creative process I had connected with this important ancestor of mine. Now having the clay piece at home makes me feel that my grandfather is somehow present in my life.

## The Wrap-Up

Our weekly session is almost over, and I give students the homework assignment that I've discussed in greater detail on my blog: describe a moment of clarity or insight.

"Have a good week," I bid the group. As they pack up their things and move toward the door, couples and small groups form, chatting about everything from writing topics to the latest antidepressant to movie and book suggestions. Many make their way to the building's garden café for more talk under the trees. Tom, our first-time class member, tells me, "Thank you. I'll be back!" and I'm pleased to see that the group invites him along for coffee.

## What Makes Writing Groups for Depression Special?

Writers tend to migrate toward writing groups. Developing writers in every genre are encouraged by their mentors to find a group of like-minded people who love to write and to meet with them regularly to share stories, chapters, articles, and poems. This is a key component of a writer's development. In response to the shared material, the other group members in a typical writing group offer feedback on what aspects of the work they liked or felt needed improvement, such as clarification, more detail, or less repetition. This reciprocal critique is how writers learn the techniques of the craft, improve their work, and perhaps move toward publication.

*I like the camaraderie of hearing others' writing, even though I'm frustrated with my writing [right now] . . . [I]t gives me the hope that someday I will again be able to have the euphoric feeling of creating words nested together exactly as they are destined to be.*

—RAIN

Writing groups for people with depression are different. In my group, positive feedback to others is encouraged, but critical comments are not allowed (except in instances when the writer specifically requests suggestions). We have the specific experience of depression in common and we are working to heal. It can be liberating to find our own voices and to explore different approaches, but polishing a piece of writing for publication is a minor goal.

Those of us with depression are managing several unique issues and working to confront them in a healing manner. First, we are in, or have been through, a debilitating depression, whether due to a significant event or a medical condition. We may have been through other traumas, too—sometimes these are the triggers of our depressed state. So we may be working to understand the meaning of these events as well as our reactions to them. In addition, we may be writing during periods of extreme distress, be it depression, anxiety, sorrow, anger, slight mania, or confused thinking. We know that these conditions can become chronic, with an acute episode coming at any time. For the seriously depressed, there are always the specters of more painful and isolating symptoms, more treatments, hospitalization, even coping with ideas of self-harm or suicide.

Ultimately, some of these factors often join to profoundly affect the self-image of all writers with depression. Our self-esteem may be weak because of negative self-talk or the stigmatizing behavior of those around us. And all of these issues mean that a group for a *general* population of writers may not feel safe, at least initially. Our journeys to ease our depression will involve facing inner issues for the most part; the path of the critique group members is focused on improving the literary quality of their work.

## Benefits of Peer Support for Depression

Confiding in another person with depression—someone who has "been there"—can be greatly comforting and even empowering. Author William Styron, in his memoir *Darkness Visible* (Random House, 1990), described how a good friend—a "celebrated newspaper columnist"—who was recovering from bipolar disorder, called nearly every day during Styron's months of decline into deep depression. The friend gave support and advice when

Styron became suicidal and when he was afraid of going to the hospital. Styron wrote: "His support was unending and priceless. . . . I still look back on his concern with immense gratitude."[1] And the friend also benefited from this two-way relationship, Styron explained: "The help [my friend] gave me, he later said, had been a continuing therapy for him, thus demonstrating that, if nothing else, the disease engenders lasting fellowship."[2]

In addition to such fruitful one-on-one relationships, fellowship is found in many peer-led support groups for people with depression around the United States. Such support groups (not to be confused with writing groups) offer education on the condition, resources for finding treatment, a place to ask questions and share experiences, guidance and assistance in making plans for recovery from depression, a friendly sounding board, and the camaraderie of others. Among other organizations, peer support groups are operated by the National Alliance on Mental Illness and by the Depression and Bipolar Support Alliance, two large education and advocacy groups. The leaders, who are themselves living with one of these mood disorders, facilitate groups at community mental health centers, clinics, hospitals, homeless shelters, and other sites.

Numerous research studies on the efficacy of peer support groups show that they are powerful parts of a depression treatment program. Measurable changes associated with attending a group include the following:[3]

- Improvement in symptoms

- Fewer hospitalizations

- A decrease in the length of hospital stays

- Larger social support networks

- Enhanced self-esteem and social functioning

- Greater improvement in well-being (including recovery, quality of life, meaning of life, and hope)

While no one has yet qualitatively measured the effects of *writing* in a peer group for depression, the support it offers is undeniable. Let's look at some of the ways my group and I have observed and experienced mental health improvements.

## Benefits of a Peer Writing Group for Depression

After years of leading writing groups for my peers with depression or bipolar disorder, I've concluded that the most important thing we accomplish is to build self-esteem. Your opinion of yourself may diminish when you become depressed; I know mine does. The negative messages we're likely to send ourselves when deeply depressed, as well as the negative stigma often attached to these ailments by the people around us, can destroy our sense of worth in many ways. But I believe that some of the unique qualities of a writing group for depression can go a long way toward healing our feelings of worth, and thus easing depression, in several ways, as described below.

*I am proud as others read their thoughts and I feel grateful they have a safe place to come. I like to see when friendships are made and when we smile or nod at each other after reading. The bond exists because there is no one judging.*

—KATHERINE

- **Community building**. Writing, reading aloud, and listening in a peer group provides reassurance that you are not alone with your experiences around depression, that your experiences are real. Here you find people you can connect with even in the face of the isolation that is a frequent symptom of depression. Finding such a community can provide great relief, have a calming effect, and help increase social functioning.

- **Increased insight**. Writing about your depression and the traumas and difficulties that can surround it can be very clarifying. Research indicates that by developing new perspectives and by constructing a narrative—two common writing techniques we work on—emotional healing takes place. By creating a narrative, we are forced to organize and integrate our thoughts and feelings. By expressing ourselves in these new structures, and by listening to others, we come to realize that our unique tales ring true with others and represent universal truths. These groups also help us find our own writer's voice. I recall one member who, for many months, laughingly complained, "I don't have anything to say" to every writing prompt. She would write a bit and repeat herself a lot. But, given time and encouragement from the group, she persevered and did, to her great pleasure, eventually discover and begin to use her own voice and her own memories and ideas.

- **Sense of accomplishment**. Creating anything, whether through writing or other activities, whether alone or in a group, tends to lead to a sense of pride. "I feel good when I make something out of nothing," members often report. Especially after a barren period of depression, writing can be empowering, and this in turn may lead to further creative activities and steps toward recovery.

- **Unconditional acceptance**. When reading our writing aloud, we should always feel that we are being honored by the group's attention and that our work is respected. This recognition and validation of ourselves and our stories is needed by every writer but can be especially valuable in this situation because it is often sadly lacking for those coping with depression.

- **Engendering compassion**. By listening to and supporting others in the group, we demonstrate caring. This empowers others and decreases their feelings of isolation. Many people living with various serious illnesses report that helping others who are ill is an intensely healing process for them as well.

- **Developing writing skills**. Most people who join a writing group for depression don't aspire to become professional writers. Healing is their goal. However, as we strive to precisely describe memories, ideas, feelings, and stories, these things become clearer in our minds. With every new technique learned, every exercise completed, we seem to process and heal further. Thus, in addition to developing new coping mechanisms through writing skills, you may discover a creative outlet that you utilize in other venues, or—who knows?—even a vocation.

## A Unique Environment

You learned in chapter 2 that a writing group for depression is *not* group therapy, though it may be therapeutic. In this chapter, you've read about how a writing group for depression is *not* a critique group. While it has some of the advantages of a general peer support group, it offers its own distinct means of healing by increasing insight and a sense of accomplishment while creating a community that models unconditional acceptance and compassion for others.

All of these factors mean that in a peer writing group for depression, self-esteem can be fed and nurtured along with writing skills. We've watched as people with depression write through their grief over the death of a parent, through the pain and anger of divorce, and through coming to terms with severe childhood abuses. Listening as their writing changes over weeks and months is inspiring, as is watching one member leave for a newfound career, another for an active volunteer position. We are a caring and cohesive bunch. It's clear when you notice both soothing voices and laughter over coffee after the meeting; it's clear when members throw a surprise party for me.

*to write*

### A HEALING ACTION

**What is one specific thing you've done to help heal your depression? It might be habitual or a onetime event. Describe the action and how it made you feel.**

In this exercise, Samantha wrote in response to the prompt "fire," and shared with the group a healing ritual for releasing past traumas.

**ANOTHER VOICE**

### *Fire* by Samantha

It was really difficult to get the fire started. It was windy by the lake, and I worried that my ambitious plan to burn away the pain of my past, in this place of power and beauty, would be thwarted—put on the back burner, if you will—by the elements.

It was just yesterday, at Lake Shasta. It [might] have been a month ago that, on the advice of an intuitive healer, I wrote down all of the painful, dysfunctional, destructive things I had learned in the past. She had told me to write about my mother, and to be sure, that took the lion's share of the four journal pages—but there was some pretty potent stuff left to me by my father and exes, too. They were all things that I knew I should—even [had] to—let go of, to become the person I know I am capable of becoming, but somehow just haven't been able to do.

We started in the middle of the lake, on a paddle boat. But maybe we would have been caught by the patrolling sheriffs if the pages had caught flame, because we went through two-thirds of the matchbook without even touching fire to paper.

And so we tried again—paddled to shore, got in the car, went looking for a quiet, private, beautiful space where I could perform my purification ritual. I fought against the voices contained in those pages as we drove—a litany of pessimism, hopelessness, powerlessness, worthlessness. "This isn't going to work. I can't do anything right. Maybe it's not supposed to work. I'll never be free. . . . I don't deserve to be free."

But as always happens when perseverance outlives pessimism, I did in fact succeed.

It looked like a white rose while it burned. The past is now ashes, and I feel so free. Just as a forest fire destroys, and in destruction wipes the earth clean, readying it for new life[, so] burning the inheritance of my depression could be the fresh start I'm looking for.

This Phoenix will rise from the ashes of the pages that were my past.

*to write*

## FINDING SUPPORT IN A GROUP

Have you ever been part of a supportive group of people—a sports team, a group of friends, a religious congregation? Freewrite on who you were with, how you came together, how you demonstrated support for each other, and how it felt.

# *Developing a Writing Group for People with Depression*

How can you develop your own peer writing group for people with depression? First of all, clear guidelines are needed. Second, a leader or facilitator who possesses certain qualities and knowledge is required. Third, you must recruit participants. Here I'll describe what has worked best in my group at Stanford over the years and offer suggestions as to how you might go about creating such a community. Please keep in mind that most of these guidelines will work equally well for a group of people with less severe depressions.

# *Clear Guidelines Are Crucial*

Several important guidelines keep the group an emotionally and physically safe place for everyone and allow each person to grow as a writer and to heal. These are described briefly here and discussed in more detail in following sections.

- **Confidentiality**. Writers often share very personal information in the group, and it must be understood that whatever goes on in the meeting room stays in the room. There must be agreement from each person, in writing, as soon as he or she joins the group that no content of the group is discussed outside. This provides an environment in which people feel emotionally secure about reading and speaking.

- **Respect for one another**. Criticizing or interrupting another writer is not acceptable. Each person's turn to read or speak is honored, and attention from the group is expected. Giving advice is also not appropriate. If a reader specifically asks the group for advice, any discussions should take place after the meeting.

- **Emotional safety**. As I've stated, no one should ever feel pressured to read his or her writing aloud in this type of group; it is always acceptable to simply pass when it is your turn. For those who do read, it's important to emphasize that writing is not critiqued in a workshop for depression. Instead, listeners are encouraged to offer specific, positive feedback on writing, if they are so moved. If members cry while reading, they are quietly invited to take a moment to compose themselves and then finish reading if possible. If they choose, they may ask another person to finish reading for them, or simply stop if necessary.

> *Writing is an incomparable tool for empowerment. . . . [W]riting can be the bridge out of isolation into community. In community there can be hope and help.*
>
> —PAT SCHNEIDER, *Writing Alone and with Others*

- **Physical safety and well-being**. Because writers in this type of group are coping with depression, they may be especially vulnerable to the emotions that can be awakened by writing, reading, and listening. Although I've found it to be a very rare problem, if a writer's demeanor or the content of her writing suggests that her safety or well-being is at risk, the leader must tactfully but directly ask that person to talk with her briefly after the group meeting. If a writer appears to be at risk of harming herself and cannot complete the meeting, the leader should talk with her alone outside the room to determine together what action should be taken. (See "When a Writer Is at Risk" below.)

# *Qualities of a Workshop Leader*

Four attributes are required for a leader of a writing group for people with depression: some knowledge of mood disorders, including signs that someone is at risk; some knowledge of writing; experience facilitating groups; and the dedication and ability to apply these appropriately to enable healing. As part of this, the leader must write and read along with the rest of the group. This last point is important, because it builds trust and community among the writers—everyone is on common ground, exploring ideas and emotions together. It also enables the leader to grow as a writer and to heal during the meeting, too.

When I proposed and began leading the group at Stanford, I possessed some of each of these: in addition to my personal experiences with bipolar depression, I had read extensively on mood disorders and attended numerous seminars and peer groups; I had studied creative writing and worked as a professional journalist, writer, and editor; I had facilitated peer support groups and I had experience teaching both biology and creative writing; I was sensitive enough to be gentle and encouraging, but firm; and I was excited about sharing the techniques that had helped me so much.

Every leader will have a different background—and there is an enormous range of training possibilities for a peer leader of a writing group for depression. For example, education and preparation for working with peers with mood disorders in a variety of ways is available from both the National Alliance on Mental Illness and the Depression and Bipolar Support Alliance. Knowledge of and experience in the field of creative writing can be obtained in many ways. While a group leader need not be a published writer, she should have at least some training from creative writing classes or workshops so that she can create or find appropriate prompts for the group in the three categories described earlier: warm-up exercises, exploration exercises, and reflection exercises.

When I began the Stanford group, I was unaware that there was anyone else doing this type of work. In fact, an organization, the National

Association for Poetry Therapy (NAPT), has been evolving since the 1960s. Today there are several excellent organizations that offer writing-and-healing workshops for specialized groups of people, and their methods for training leaders vary. For example, the Center for Journal Therapy as well as the Amherst Writers and Artists program both offer training of writers who wish to facilitate workshops with general and very specific groups of people. In addition, the National Federation for Biblio/Poetry Therapy—a branch of the NAPT—now offers training to become a certified poetry therapist or a registered poetry therapist. Both of these designations require training in psychology in addition to training in literature and professional practice; the second requires at least a master's degree in a mental health field.

A mental health care professional without depression, who is also trained in some form of creative writing or writing therapy, would be a good candidate to lead a writing workshop for depressed people, too. However, I do not believe that a formal mental health care background is required, as long as the peer leader possesses the other necessary qualities and knowledge, and follows appropriate guidelines. In fact, as discussed above, peer support itself is often a very powerful aid to healing from depression.

## Giving Feedback

Just as reading aloud is optional, so is receiving feedback; a writer can always specify that he would like the group to "listen only." This still allows the writer to benefit from hearing his own work aloud and having it witnessed by others. For other cases, specific positive comments on the piece can be offered after a member reads (for example, "I liked the description of the river at dusk," "That metaphor felt perfect," "You created a very intriguing character," or "Your use of humor was wonderful"). If no feedback is forthcoming from the group, the leader can offer her own reflections on the piece or simply say, "Thank you for sharing that," to the writer. Group members should be reminded that getting no feedback is not a sign that the writing was somehow poor; sometimes listeners are so moved by a piece that they can't immediately respond.

## Truth or Fiction?

In some writing groups I've been a part of, all writing is presumed to be fictional unless the author chooses to state otherwise. This policy sometimes frees writers to write more expansively or to reveal more intimate material than they might otherwise do, since they do not need to claim personal material as their own in front of the group. Instead, comments can refer to "the narrator" rather than "you."

Whenever I have discussed instituting this rule with the group at Stanford, there has been strong group consensus against it. Members have argued that the rule would impede empathy, support, and community formation in this environment and is unnecessary since members already know that depression is common to all of them. In addition, they have felt that their privacy is already protected by the confidentiality agreement. Finally, group members have expressed concern that if we used the fiction rule, we might not be aware when someone is feeling particularly vulnerable or even at risk. Hence, in our group it has worked well to treat works as autobiographical unless we are specifically setting out to write fiction together.

> *No one, no matter how many degrees he has, how much she's published, how many awards she has, or how much money he makes, has the right to treat another human being with disrespect.*
>
> —Judy Reeves, *Writing Alone, Writing Together*

## When a Writer Is at Risk

What happens in the extreme situation when a writer seems to be expressing her thoughts or intentions of harming or killing herself? This has been an extremely rare experience for me, but a group leader must be prepared for the strong emotions that can arise. It's important for a peer leader to be supportive in this situation but also to clearly maintain the position of being a writing group leader, not a mental health care professional.

I have found it best to say, "I'm glad you shared with us how you're feeling. Can you and I talk together about this situation after the group?" At that time, I can ask the writer privately if she currently feels confident she is safe from self-harm. Even if she does, I still encourage the writer to contact her mental health care provider about the strong feelings she experienced. I've never had an instance in which a writer was in such crisis that she did not feel safe from self-harm, but I would insist that she get immediate help from a professional or go to the emergency room in such a situation. Also, when registering for the group, writers provide their professional's name and phone number and indicate in writing that I have their permission to call that professional in an emergency. If I felt the writer was not willing to seek immediate help in such a situation, I would contact her physician or therapist directly.

## *The Presentation of Prompts*

The writing group leader must be very aware of each prompt's effects on people. When a topic, usually in an "exploration" exercise, is likely to evoke very difficult emotions, I often offer an alternate topic (although group members are also always free to choose any topic they like to write on). An alternate topic may or may not be related to the original one but is in a lighter vein so that a writer who doesn't feel comfortable with the first topic has another option.

When formulating any prompt, the leader also needs to frame it appropriately. The goal is not to dredge up the most difficult feelings possible for these writers, but to offer something to think about that, preferably, can be explored at a variety of emotional levels. For example, rather than offering, "What opportunities have you lost to your depression?" you could suggest the more positive, "What have you learned from your experiences with depression?" or "What is one step you would like to take in your recovery from depression?" Both of these alternate prompts allow a writer to examine opportunities lost, if she chooses to, but don't force her to frame her response in those terms if that feels too painful. This reframing concept may also need to be applied when using prompts that have been put forth by other members on the "Topic Suggestions" page I circulate periodically.

## Exercises to Avoid

It is also crucial that the leader consider how certain exercises that try to evoke an "altered mental state" may affect people coping with depression and possibly other mental illnesses. In some classes I've taken, I've been presented with an "automatic writing" exercise in which we wrote with our nondominant hand and did not look at our page as we wrote. While this is purported to allow you to access otherwise unconscious material, I have found that it can be very disturbing for people coping with psychosis or dissociative disorders. Furthermore, guided imagery or guided meditation exercises, while loved by some writers, can be very frightening for those who have any tendency to dissociate. Any time I use imagery exercises, I tell writers they can simply look down, rather than close their eyes; imagine a scene, rather than "see yourself"; and I keep it brief.

## Setting Behavior Boundaries

Now and then, particularly when a new writer enters an established group, a member may dominate conversation, take feedback or discussion in an unrelated direction, or lecture a writer or the group. It's important for the leader to jump in right away in this case and teach that writer the ground rules. This is part of facilitating any type of group but is especially important when deep emotions and new artistic creations are at risk. I've sometimes had to be very firm, and even loud, in order to rein in such talkers, hopefully without embarrassing them. Often this is a matter of clearly reminding them of the format of the group. For example, I may tell them, "Now it's time for the next writer to read, so let's give her our attention" or "Let's focus on giving appropriate feedback right now; that may be a discussion for after the group." This type of behavior usually disappears after the person has participated in one or two sessions and understands the format and expectations.

When a writing group includes those dealing with the depressed phase of bipolar disorder, it is possible to occasionally have a hypomanic (overactive or slightly manic) member at a meeting. (Truly manic members typically can't sit still in the room for long, so their presence is unlikely.) In this case, it's important for the leader to identify what specific behaviors are problematic and guide the person to more appropriate alternatives that don't disrupt the group. This is usually a matter of discouraging too much irrelevant talking. However, if a member is unable to sit still but fidgets during writing exercises to the point of disturbing others, he should be tactfully told of this. If it continues, the leader may want to talk with him outside of the room and explain the problem, offering that if he can't control these symptoms now, he'll need to leave but is very welcome to return the following week when he is feeling more even.

Group members sometimes write about past psychotic breaks (experiencing hallucinations or delusions), which are very important for them to process and understand. However, I've found that people currently in a mild psychotic phase of depression or mania, and people with schizophrenia, typically find a group meeting uncomfortable and do not tend to stay in the group very long.

## When a Leader Is Unavailable

Here are a few very practical points: in order to prepare for a situation in which I am ill or away, I maintain an e-mail list of writing group members and contact them with as much warning as possible that a meeting will be cancelled. An alternative is to gradually train a co-leader or assistant leader who can take over in such a case.

I also try to continue posting writing exercises on my blog at least once a week when I am away from the group for any reason. While I encourage writers to check it for homework and other assignments even when we are meeting regularly, this is also a good way to help them keep up their writing practice and their connection to the group when we are not meeting.

## Recruiting Writing Group Members

I began recruiting writers for the Stanford group by simply posting color-ful fliers around the psychiatry clinic offering "Creative Writing for People with Mood Disorders." I still use these today, ten years later, but now the group is also advertised in many support groups, the county mental health centers, and the local NAMI (National Alliance on Mental Illness) bul-letin, and is recommended by many mental health care providers to their clients and patients. The writers themselves do a lot of advertising by word of mouth, too. All of these options are great means of letting people know of your group, and of course, the group will tend to build momentum over time. I find that a group of at least four writers is a good size in order to build a true group dynamic (although by all means you could write with just one or two friends who have depression—this may even feel the safest to start). However, we now typically number about fourteen writers per session, and even this large number is workable.

Another way of forming a group is to use an existing depression *support* group and designate one meeting a month to be a writing day. An addi-tional option is to form a writing group online for people with depression. You could, for example, offer this option at a general writing-forum website and see if this specialty is of interest to existing writers, who can then form a subgroup. Some writing websites of interest, as well as mental health web-sites, are listed in the *Bibliography and Selected Resources* section.

## Screening Writers for the Group

The fliers I use to advertise my group contain a short description of my background in terms of education and writing and the fact that I use creative writing to help manage my own bipolar disorder. It tells when the group meets, and in what building, but does not indicate the room number; then it indicates that to register, you should call me, and it gives my business phone number (*not* my home number). This information allows potential writers to see whether they feel generally interested in the group but requires them to call in order for me to register them and give them detailed directions and the room number. In this way I can screen applicants, as well as answer their questions about the group before they arrive at their first meeting.

When I speak with a potential group member, I ascertain whether she has a mood disorder (required for participation), whether she is under the care of a mental health professional (required for those with medical diagnoses only, not situational depression), and whether she feels stable enough to participate (that is, not presently psychotic or suicidal). If her responses indicate she is appropriate for the group, I obtain her contact information and indicate that she'll be asked to sign a waiver at her first meeting. This form includes her agreement with our confidentiality rule and her understanding that I, the leader, am *not* a mental health care professional.

## Where to Meet and How to Pay for It

Unless you are planning a small writing group of people you know well, I don't recommend that you meet in anyone's home. I wouldn't suggest this in any case, regardless of whether the group members are dealing with depression or not, for reasons of personal safety. Instead, try to obtain a meeting space at a clinic, hospital, or mental health center. Those that also offer depression support groups are probably your best bet. Other options include community centers, libraries, coffeehouses, or even restaurants (if it's during a slow period and you eat, too). You can also investigate where local twelve-step programs have their meetings, since these places may be amenable to another group.

Hopefully you can find a site that doesn't charge for its use or has a minimal fee that the writers' donations—of as little as a dollar or two each—could cover. (These optional donations can be collected in a passed envelope, or placed into a container at the door. No one should be turned away for an inability to donate.) While a writing *class* charges tuition fees, I believe that a peer writing group should not. If a teacher is teaching, she should of course charge her students; if she is leading, as a *peer*, she should either be paid by a hosting organization or lead as a volunteer. This is important because it maintains equality and a sense of peers working in community within the group. Furthermore, the group may include members who are seriously ill and are unable to work and therefore live largely or solely on mental health disability payments; they may not be able to afford fees and would be deprived of the healing benefits of a writing group if they had to pay a tuition fee.

## A Healing Experience

Developing and leading a peer writing group for people with depression can be a growing experience for you, too. If you feel drawn to such work with others, you have probably already felt the healing power of writing, and of sharing and facilitating, in your own life. By leading, you continue to ease your own depression, and you are helped by helping others.

Furthermore, if you are also a writer, this can be an excellent addition to your schedule—weekly writing sessions, designing writing prompts, weekly blogging on related topics, and meeting regularly with other writers. Even during very depressed weeks, leading the group at Stanford has provided me with healthy structure and enjoyable obligations to meet. When I'm feeling better, it helps me keep my mind focused on the writing I want to accomplish both in and outside of the group session.

*to write*

## LEADING A GROUP

Do you feel any interest in leading a writing group for people with depression? Freewrite about any experience you've had leading groups before—whether it was a business meeting or taking a few friends on a hike. How was it rewarding and how was it difficult? And how might you apply what you learned there to leading a new group like this?

# Chapter 14

# *Writing On: More Exercises, Ideas, and Advice for Your Journey*

*Follow your bliss and doors will open where
there were no doors before.*

—JOSEPH CAMPBELL, *The Power of Myth*

As I write this, my illness has steadied considerably, and it's been more than four years since I've had ECT. This is largely thanks to a new experimental treatment that doctors encouraged me to try: TMS, or transcranial magnetic stimulation. Using a magnetic device held against the side of my head, a machine delivers powerful, precise magnetic pulses to a spot above my right temple—a brain area thought to be sluggish during bipolar depression. The treatment requires no anesthetic and only causes an occasional headache; I don't discern any memory loss. And for me it has worked wonders: for more than three years, I've consistently recovered within a few weeks from the suicidal depressions that still suddenly engulf me at times, no matter how well life is going. Between these cycles, I can function at almost full capacity with just my ever-present cocktail of meds.

My husband, John, and I are thrilled with this improvement, of course. Gradually I feel I'm gaining much of my life back. In fact, we recently concluded that parenting is an option for us: we have decided to adopt a child and expect to be proud parents of a toddler-aged girl next year. I can hardly wait to write about her.

I continue to write nearly every day. My book-length memoir of my illness is nearly complete, and I contemplate publishing it. Numerous other writing projects are in the works. Putting down my thoughts and feelings and ideas still provides me with a sense of calm and control that little else does, and the joy of creating keeps me feeling alive, even when I occasionally feel dark despair pressing on my mind and body. I'm profoundly thankful for all the medical treatments that have helped me to varying degrees over the years. Yet the call of words has healed me, too. At times, writing has saved my life.

\* \* \* \*

Years ago, when I began writing to ease my depression, I also discovered my bliss—writing brought me a new way of thinking and feeling and being in the world. Now it is one of my mainstays, and it continues to bring me joy. Perhaps the blessing, as well as the burden, of depression is that it leads to changes.

If you love writing and find that it indeed eases your depression, keep at it. Learn constantly by reading and listening and talking with other writers in order to keep those benefits and that excitement fresh.

But whether writing itself is your "bliss" or not, I hope that it can be a *tool* to help you find your own bliss as you cope with your depression. In order to discover more about yourself and how you would like things to change in your life, write about it. Write about your depression and see what you can learn from that, but also write about those things you've always wanted to do—and how you can take a step toward making one of them happen. Write about coping strategies—and also about what intrigues you, what you love, what you want to experiment with. Consider the real world, but let yourself dream in your writing, too.

I hope that the techniques in this book have given you the implements with which to explore whatever it is your intuition tells you to investigate, whether it's through a love poem to your child, your own history, freewriting about a job you'd like to try, or a story about a character finding new perspectives on life. So, keep writing—turn to writing when you need a chance to think more clearly or to find encouragement or to learn what you want to do next.

Researcher James W. Pennebaker, who pioneered work in the writing-and-healing field summarized: "Writing therapy isn't a one-size-fits-all. . . . [I]f you want to write, just sit down and write! . . . It's okay to experiment with new ways. Write a lot of ways! And let the writing heal you."[1]

You are your own best guide in terms of what exactly in your mind and heart needs to be dusted off with those archeologist's brushes, so choose writing topics you like or need. The rest of this chapter also offers a lot of ideas to point you in new directions and keep you going. These are exercises that I've used successfully myself or in my group. You'll find them listed in several categories below, and there are suggestions in the *Bibliography and Selected Resources* section on places to find additional ideas.

Most of all, I hope that you will return again and again to writing to help you as you cope with your depression. Remember to work to build a writing habit, but do not let yourself be daunted by writing when you feel depressed. Do what you can do and try again the next day and the next and you will build your writing momentum. Explore your inner life and your outer world freely, and enjoy finding your voice and creating art on your writing journey. Word by word you will find your way, learning what heals you and eases your depression. Happy writing and good health.

## Explorations

These exercises fall mainly into the category of "exploration questions." Write for twenty minutes on the questions in the first paragraph. Next, read the "Then consider this" paragraph and use it to reflect on what you've discovered by writing for another five minutes.

## to write

### AN "AHA!" MOMENT

Describe a time you felt a moment of clarity or insight, a flash of understanding, or that feeling of "Why didn't I think of that before?"

Then consider this: Was the flash you described useful for you? If so, are there any ways you could replicate the situation in order to invite more such insights?

## to write

### BEING OUTSIDE

Are you a forest person, a desert person, a mountain person—or do you prefer to sit in the living room with a book? (That's okay, too.) Choose some type of outdoor environment and write continuously, beginning with "In a forest, I am. . . ." (Fill in whatever word is appropriate for the site you have in mind.) This might be a spot you love or hate or are afraid in, one you're near every day, or one you dream of visiting.

Then consider this: How does it feel to write about this location? What can you do to feel emotionally well based on this writing? Does it confirm that you're a contented indoor type who despises mosquitoes or does it trigger ideas about where to stroll this afternoon or camp this weekend?

## to write

### CAFFEINE AND ALCOHOL

Write about your feelings about caffeine and/or alcohol. Do you use either—why or why not? Have they affected your depression or other parts of your life?

Then consider this: Has your attitude toward them changed with your depression and its treatments? And would you like to change your intake patterns for either?

## *to write*

### RESPONSIBILITY

Write continuously on the topic of "responsibility" and what it means to you—whether it's about a babysitter you trust or protesting for civil rights or taking proper care of your mental and physical health.

Then consider this: What do your thoughts and feelings on this topic indicate about you? For example, do you feel overly responsible for things outside your control? Do you tend to shirk duties? Are there ways you could adjust "responsibility" in your life and improve your mood in the process?

## *to write*

### ON PARENTS

Choose one parent or guardian and describe your past and present relationship with that person. Try to incorporate at least a couple of specific stories or events.

Then consider this: How has this person supported and encouraged you? Even if the relationship has been difficult, do you feel thankful for some of your interactions? How might you like to improve your view of that relationship today—for example, could you recognize your separateness and release some frustration or pain? Are there areas you'd like to build on?

## *to write*

### BELONGING TO "CLUB MEDS"

If you take medication for your depression, bipolar disorder, or other mental health condition, how did you feel when you started it? Did you resist at all or welcome it with open arms? Why?

Then consider this: Have your feelings changed at all over time? How does your attitude toward your medicine affect you and your condition today?

*to write*

## IS THERE A BOOK IN YOU?

Imagine you were to sit down at the kitchen table and start writing or typing your first book. What would it be about? What would you really like to say to the world and leave behind in perpetuity?

Then consider this: What does your book topic tell you about what is important to you? Does your enthusiasm for writing about the ocean suggest you might want to spend more time at the beach? If you felt inclined to write a memoir, what events in your life would you like to get on paper?

*to write*

## PICTURING YOURSELF

Imagine you are creating a character for a novel and that character is based on you. How will you describe this character for brand-new readers? How do you envision your own size, shape, color? What about your talents, skills, and weaknesses and your faith, maturity, and sense of justice? Describe this person—yourself—as objectively as possible.

Then consider this: Are there things you'd like to adjust, whether by modifying something about yourself or by simply deciding to look at something in a new light? (Later, the opinion of a trusted friend or therapist might be valuable if you're interested in making changes in your self-image.)

*to write*

## SPIRITUALITY'S ROLE IN DEPRESSION

We all have views of ourselves, of how the world operates, and of the mysteries life offers, and the way we envision these things defines our spirituality. Describe your spiritual views and how they relate to your depression. For example, does being an atheist ground you when you're ill? Does your belief in God help you keep going despite your symptoms? And have your depression experiences changed your worldview?

Then consider this: what did you find? Exploring spirituality with respect to your depression may make you more consciously aware of your beliefs and may even provide you with a lifeline when difficult thoughts and painful feelings strike.

*to write*

## ROMANCE

Write about someone in your romantic life—for example, your spouse, partner, a current or former relationship, or your ideal relationship— and his or her relationship to your mental health. Does that person know about your depression or bipolar disorder? Can you discuss it with him or her? Is that person supportive?

Then consider this: Does reading what you wrote provide insight into changes you might like to make in this realm, if any? Does it suggest any conversations you would like to have?

*to write*

## THE STIGMA AROUND DEPRESSION

As a result of your depression, you may have heard frustrating comments from some of those around you: "She's just not trying," "He's just got an attitude problem." Describe any stigmatization you've felt as a result of your illness. Who has it come from? In what form? How did you feel as a result?

Then consider this: Could you brainstorm to find things that might help you cope with this? How could you educate people who make such remarks?

# *Quotations to Use as Writing Prompts*

Choose a quotation and write for twenty minutes in response to it as a whole, or to a sentence, phrase, or word that attracts you.

*Getting better [from depression] means taking risks. The first risks I took*
*were physical, like starting ballet classes at age [thirty-seven]. Then,*
*I took emotional ones. I began expressing my thoughts. I joined a support*
*group. I made new friends. If there is something good for you that*
*feels emotionally risky, try writing it down. Sometimes seeing it*
*in print gives you courage.*

—Julia Thorne, *You Are Not Alone*

*I'm a great believer in luck and I find the harder I work,*
*the more I have of it.*

—George Bernard Shaw

*We must learn to see the world anew.*

—Albert Einstein

*Seek out that particular mental attribute which makes you feel most*
*deeply and vitally alive, along with which comes the inner voice which says,*
*"This is the real me," and when you have found that attitude, follow it.*

—William James

*Man often becomes what he believes himself to be.*
*If I keep on saying to myself that I cannot do a certain thing,*
*it is possible that I may end by really becoming incapable of doing it.*
*On the contrary, if I have the belief that I can do it, I shall surely acquire*
*the capacity to do it even if I may not have it at the beginning.*

—Mahatma Gandhi

*I felt like I'd been found incompetent and fired from my own life*
*[during my depression].*

—Darcey Steinke, in *Unholy Ghost*

*Push yourself beyond when you think you are done with what you have*
*to say. Go a little further. Sometimes when you think you are done,*
*it is just the edge of beginning. Probably that's why we decide we're done.*
*It's getting too scary. . . . It is beyond the point when you think you*
*are done that often something strong comes out.*

—Natalie Goldberg, *Writing Down the Bones*

*Knowing others is wisdom; knowing the self is enlightenment.*

—*Tao Te Ching*

*There is a vitality, a life-force, an energy, a quickening that is translated*
*through you into action, and because there is only one of you in*
*all of time, this expression is unique. And if you block it, it will never exist*
*through any other medium and will be lost. The world will not have it!*
*It is not your business to determine how good it is nor how it compares with*
*other expressions. It is your business to keep it yours clearly*
*and directly, to keep the channel open.*

—Martha Graham

*Leap, and the net will appear.*

—Julia Cameron, *The Vein of Gold*

*To dare is to lose one's footing temporarily; to not dare is to lose one's life.*

—Søren Kierkegaard

*Aware of my mental health, I breathe in.*
*Smiling to my state of mental health, I breathe out.*

—Thich Nhat Hanh

## Sentence Stems

The sentence stems listed below are some favorites of mine. Choose one and write for twenty minutes, beginning with that stem. Use the stem once or return to it many times in your writing. Make up some of your own sentence stems, too.

- In a forest (desert, mountain range), I feel . . .
- I used to believe that . . .
- If only I had . . .
- An occupation I'd love to try is . . .
- In kindergarten I thought . . .
- When I traveled to . . .
- Today I'm feeling . . .
- Looking back, it's clear that . . .
- If only I weren't so scared . . .
- If I were rich beyond dreams . . .
- When I swallow my depression medicine, I feel . . .
- I always thought . . .
- It's so annoying when . . .
- Tomorrow I will . . .
- It's so comforting when . . .
- The person I'd like to ask for help is . . .
- I'd like to invent . . .
- The best music I ever heard was . . .
- I'm disappointed when . . .
- When I glanced at the clock . . .
- My favorite thing about myself is . . .

- It thrills me when . . .
- I'm so thankful for . . .
- The person I most admire is . . .
- On a perfect day I would . . .
- I hate it when . . .
- She/he let me down when . . .
- I anticipate that . . .
- I was about to make my escape when . . .
- My strategy is to . . .

# Poems to Use as Prompts

This list includes some of my favorite poems to use as writing prompts, but be sure to look for others you like by paging through any poetry anthology. Write in response to the ideas in the poem or in response to a word, phrase, or sentence. Or write a letter to the poet in response. Write either in prose or in the form of a poem. (Most of these poems may be found in the individual author's collections; some websites containing large poetry collections are listed in the *Bibliography and Selected Resources* section.)

- "Morning," "My Life," and "To a Stranger Born in Some Distant Country Hundreds of Years from Now" by Billy Collins
- "'Hope' is the thing with feathers" by Emily Dickinson
- "Prayer" by C. P. Estes
- "Gift" by Judith Hemschemeyer
- "Back," "Having it Out with Melancholy," "Pardon," and "Waiting" by Jane Kenyon
- "Grasshoppers," "A Happy Birthday," "The Necktie," "Skater," and "Tectonics" by Ted Kooser

- "Dust" by Dorianne Laux

- "Candles in Babylon" by Denise Levertov

- "Gift" by Czeslaw Milosz

- "Remember" by Wayne Muller

- "The Esquimos Have No Word for 'War,'" "The Journey," "Wild Geese," and "Morning Poem" by Mary Oliver

- "To Have without Holding" by Marge Piercy

- "You Ask Me Why I Make My Home in the Mountain Forest" by Li Po

- "The Guest House" by Rumi

- "The Zen of Housework" by Al Zolynas

## *More Prompts*

Here is a grab bag of additional prompts that we've used in my group; some were created by other group members. (Writing about pets is always extremely popular, these prompts have shown me, as is writing on love and what we call "The Big Questions," such as the first two listed here.)

- Who do you think you are?
- What is reality anyway?
- The first pet you ever owned
- A current pet, and how it affects your mood
- Love
- Your first job
- Black velvet
- Thunderstorms
- A temptation
- A childhood illness

- Something hilarious
- Your journey through life (depression, a relationship, into the future)
- Kaleidoscopes
- Joy
- A message from your ancestors
- Math (or any other class)
- Reason
- Spiritual guidance
- A lousy cold or flu
- A childhood toy
- Tobacco
- Self-care tips you recommend for depression
- What bodily sensations do you feel right now?
- Computers
- Friends
- Where are you in "recovering" a life that is meaningful to you?
- Triangles
- The first sound (taste, sight, smell, feeling) of the day
- Tragedy
- Saying "I love you"
- A gift you've received
- A gift you've given
- The contents of your pantry
- A time when you were patient
- Benefits of depression
- The profession you know best
- Perfume
- Earthquakes (or other natural disasters)
- Chocolate

- A mentor
- A soothing place
- A person you'd like to meet
- A visit to the dentist
- Purple (or any other color)
- Watching cartoons
- Past successes
- A conversation with your brain (or any other organ)
- Fire
- Comfort food
- Your least favorite holiday (season, day of the week)
- Outer space
- Pillows and blankets
- The first time you rode a bike
- A lesson you have learned
- Illness and grace
- Structuring your day
- Money
- Pie
- Compassion
- Sore muscles
- A message from your wisest self
- The ocean
- A road trip
- Global warming
- Prayer or meditation
- A sunny day
- The invisible
- Dusting and vacuuming

- Feeling proud
- An obituary
- Beauty
- Your favorite movie (book, meal, vacation, TV show)
- What you see in the dark
- Your birth
- A daily ritual
- Magic
- A quirky relative
- Psychotherapy
- Postcards
- A pivotal moment in your life

# More Suggested Approaches

Here is a selection of additional writing activities you may want to experiment with, either alone or in a group.

- Collect interesting images from magazines, catalogues, postcards, calendars, and so on, and write about one you choose or select randomly.

- Write an unsent letter to a friend or relative, living or dead, or to historical figures, imaginary characters, your past self, or your future self.

- Find a small object you can hold in your hand and write about it; stones, leaves, feathers, shells, and desktop knick-knacks are all good.

- In a group, pass around a sheet for people to write topic suggestions on, and take turns selecting prompts from the list.

- Draw "how you feel today" or "what I wish for" or "my depression" or "my favorite place," and then write about your artwork and how it felt to create it.

- Take a walk or a drive or a bus ride, near or far, and sit somewhere you've never sat before; write on what you see there.

- Write each letter of the alphabet on a piece of paper, choose one randomly, and write on whatever comes to mind.

- In a group, have each person write a noun on a card and then pass it to the person on the right. Next, have each person write an adjective on the new card and pass it to the next person, and so on. After you receive a card with three or four words on it, take five minutes to write a short story using those words.

# Notes

## Introduction

1. "Writing About Feelings May Beat Talking," *New York Times*, March 7, 1991.

## Chapter 1

1. James W. Pennebaker, *Opening Up: The Healing Power of Confiding in Others* (New York: Avon Books, 1990), 51.

## Chapter 2

1. National Institute on Mental Health, www.nimh.nih.gov (accessed Sept. 14, 2007).

2. National Alliance on Mental Illness, www.nami.org (accessed Sept. 14, 2007).

3. Depression and Bipolar Support Alliance, www.dbsalliance.org (accessed Sept. 14, 2007).

4. Peter D. Kramer, *Against Depression* (New York: Viking, 2005), 154.

5. Depression and Bipolar Support Alliance, www.dbsalliance.org (accessed Sept. 14, 2007).

6. Saba Moussavi, Somnath Chatterji, Emese Verdes, Ajay Tandon, Vikram Patel, and Bedirhan Ustun, "Depression, Chronic Diseases, and Decrements in Health: Results from the World Health Surveys," *The Lancet* 370 (2007): 851–858.

7. Depression and Bipolar Support Alliance, www.dbsalliance.org (accessed Sept. 14, 2007).

8. Mental Health America, www.mentalhealthamerica.net (accessed Sept. 14, 2007).

9. William Stryon, *Darkness Visible* (New York: Random House, 1990), 37.

10. G. & C. Merriam Co., *Webster's New Collegiate Dictionary* (Springfield, MA: G. & C. Merriam Company, 1981), 1134.

11. Mental Health America, www.mentalhealthamerica.net (accessed Sept. 14, 2007).

12. Pat Schneider, *Writing Alone and with Others* (New York: Oxford University Press, 2003), 265.

13. Ibid., 263.

## Chapter 3

1. J. W. Pennebaker and J. R. Susman, "Disclosure of Traumas and Psychosomatic Processes," *Social Science and Medicine* 26 (1988): 327–332.

2. James W. Pennebaker, *Writing to Heal* (Oakland, CA: New Harbinger Publications, 2004), 4–5.

3. S. W. Cole, M. E. Kemeny, S. E. Taylor, and B. R. Visscher, "Accelerated Course of Human Immunodeficiency Virus Infection in Gay Men Who Conceal Their Homosexual Identity," *Psychosomatic Medicine* 58 (1996): 219–231.

4. J. W. Pennebaker and S. K. Beall, "Confronting a Traumatic Event: Toward an Understanding of Inhibition and Disease," *Journal of Abnormal Psychology* 95 (1986): 274–281.

5. Pennebaker, *Writing to Heal*, 8.

6. Ibid., 7–8.

7. Ibid., 9–10.

8. Stephen J. Lepore, and Joshua M. Smyth, eds., *The Writing Cure: How Expressive Writing Promotes Health and Emotional Well-Being* (Washington, DC: American Psychological Association, 2002), 11.

9. "Writing About Feelings May Beat Talking," *New York Times*, March 7, 1991.

10. Pennebaker, *Writing to Heal*, 8.

11. James W. Pennebaker, *Opening Up: The Healing Power of Confiding in Others* (New York: Avon, 1990), 49–51.

12. Pennebaker, *Writing to Heal*, 17–23.

13. Ibid., 31.

## Chapter 4

1. Peter D. Kramer, *Against Depression* (New York: Viking, 2005), 238.

2. Ibid., 332.

3. Margo Hornblower, "Grief and Rebirth," *Time*, July 10, 1995.

4. Graham Greene cited in Kay Redfield Jamison, *Touched with Fire: Manic-Depressive Illness and the Artistic Temperament* (New York: The Free Press, 1993), 124.

5. John Dryden, *Absalom and Achitophel* (1681), 163–164.

6. Nancy C. Andreasen, *The Creating Brain: The Neuroscience of Genius* (New York: Dana Press, 2005), 95.

7. Kay Redfield Jamison, *Touched with Fire*, 75–77.

8. Andreasen, *The Creating Brain*, 97–101.

9. Ibid., 96.

10. Ibid., 101–104.

11. Paul Verhaeghen, Jutta Joormann, and Rodney Khan, "Why We Sing the Blues: The Relation Between Self-Reflective Rumination, Mood, and Creativity," *Emotion* 5:2 (2005): 226.

12. Ibid., 231.

13. Edward Hoagland, *Unholy Ghost: Writers on Depression*, ed. Nell Casey (New York: Perennial, 2001), 58.

14. Susanna Kaysen, *Unholy Ghost: Writers on Depression*, ed. Nell Casey (New York: Perennial, 2001), 38–39.

15. Richard A. Friedman, "Connecting Depression and Artistry," *New York Times*, June 4, 2002.

16. Ibid.

17. David Karp, *Unholy Ghost: Writers on Depression*, ed. Nell Casey (New York: Perennial, 2001), 146.

18. Kramer, *Against Depression*, 238.

## Chapter 5

1. Paul S. Mueller, David J. Plevak, and Teresa A. Rummans, "Religious Involvement, Spirituality, and Medicine: Implications for Clinical Practice," *Mayo Clinic Proceedings* 76 (2001): 1225.

2. Harold Koenig, David Larson, and Michael McCollough, *Handbook for Religion and Health* (New York: Oxford University Press, 2001).

3. Jerome Stack, "Spirituality Is Not the Same as Religion," *The Journal of the California Alliance for the Mentally Ill* 8:4 (1997): 24.

4. Ibid.

## Chapter 6

1. Kathleen Adams, *The Way of the Journal* (Baltimore, MD: The Sidran Institute Press, 1998), XI.

2. James W. Pennebaker, *Writing to Heal* (Oakland, CA: New Harbinger Publications, 2004), 14.

3. Natalie Goldberg, *Wild Mind* (New York: Bantam Books, 1990), 39.

4. Pennebaker, *Writing to Heal*, 19.

## Chapter 9

1. Melanie A. Greenberg, Arthur A. Stone, and Camille B. Wortman, "Health and Psychological Effects of Emotional Disclosure: A Test of the Inhibition-Confrontation Approach," *Journal of Personality and Social Psychology* 71 (1996): 588–602.

2. James W. Pennebaker, *Writing to Heal* (Oakland, CA: New Harbinger Publications, 2004), 145.

3. Pat Schneider, *Writing Alone and with Others* (New York: Oxford University Press, 2003), 139.

4. Lesley Dormen, *Unholy Ghost: Writers on Depression*, ed. Nell Casey (New York: Perennial, 2001), 240.

## Chapter 12

1. Julia Cameron, *The Vein of Gold: A Journey to Your Creative Heart* (New York: Tarcher/Putnam, 1996), 193.

## Chapter 13

1. William Styron, *Darkness Visible: A Memoir of Madness* (New York: Random House, 1990), 77.

2. Ibid.

3. Jean Campbell and Judy Leaver, "Emerging New Practices in Organized Peer Support," *Meeting Report from the National Technical Assistance Center for State Mental Health Planning,* U.S. Department of Health and Human Services (March 17-18, 2003), 17.

## Chapter 14

1. Kathleen Adams, "Dipping into a Deep Pool: An Interview with James Pennebaker," *The Museletter*, www.journaltherapy.com (accessed November 2004).

# Bibliography and Selected Resources

If you feel you are in crisis due to depression, it's very important to see your health care provider right away. You may also find assistance by calling your local suicide hotline or the national line at **1-800-273-TALK** (1-800-273-8255). If you feel this is an emergency, call 911 or go to your nearest emergency room.

## DEPRESSION AND BIPOLAR DISORDER

### Books

Casey, Nell, ed. 2001. *Unholy Ghost: Writers on Depression*. New York: Perennial.

Castle, Lana R. 2006. *Finding Your Bipolar Muse: How to Master Depressive Droughts and Manic Floods and Access Your Creative Power*. New York: Marlowe.

Jamison, Kay Redfield. 1993. *Touched with Fire: Manic-Depressive Illness and the Artistic Temperament*. New York: The Free Press.

Kramer, Peter D. 2005. *Against Depression*. New York: Viking.

Meyers, Barbara F. 2005. *The Caring Congregation Handbook and Training Manual: Resources for Welcoming and Supporting Those with Mental Disorders and their Families into Our Congregations*. San Francisco: Will to Print Press.

Solomon, Andrew. 2001. *The Noonday Demon: An Atlas of Depression*. New York: Scribner.

Thorne, Julia. 1993. *You Are Not Alone: Words of Experience and Hope for the Journey through Depression*. New York: HarperPerennial.

### Internet Resources

www.dbsalliance.org—Depression and Bipolar Support Alliance. An excellent site for information on depression and bipolar disorder, where to find support groups, and advocacy; site offers private journaling opportunities.

www.nami.org—National Alliance on Mental Illness. Another excellent site for information on depression and bipolar disorder, finding support groups, and advocacy.

www.nimh.nih.gov—National Institute on Mental Health. The U.S. government's official organization on mental health, it includes statistics and information on illnesses and treatments.

## WRITING AND HEALING

### Books

Bolton, Gillie. 1999. *The Therapeutic Potential of Creative Writing*. Philadelphia: Jessica Kingsley Publishers.

Bolton, Gillie, Victoria Field, and Kate Thompson, eds. 2006. *Writing Works: A Resource Handbook for Therapeutic Writing Workshops and Activities*. Philadelphia: Jessica Kingsley Publishers.

Bolton, Gillie, Stephanie Howlett, Colin Lago, and Jeannie K. Wright, eds. 2004. *Writing Cures: An Introductory Handbook of Writing in Counseling and Therapy*. New York: Brunner-Routledge.

Bray, Sharon. 2004. *A Healing Journey: Writing Together through Breast Cancer*. Amherst, MA: Amherst Writers & Artists Press.

Bray, Sharon A. 2006. *When Words Heal: Writing through Cancer*. Berkeley, CA: Frog, Ltd.

DeSalvo, Louise. 1999. *Writing as a Way of Healing*. Boston: Beacon Press.

Klauser, Henriette Anne. 2003. *With Pen in Hand: The Healing Power of Writing*. Cambridge, MA: Perseus.

Kominars, Shepard B. 2007. *Write for Life: Healing Body, Mind, and Spirit through Journal Writing*. Cleveland, OH: Cleveland Clinic Press.

Lepore, Stephen J., and Joshua M. Smyth, eds. 2002. *The Writing Cure: How Expressive Writing Promotes Health and Emotional Well-Being*. Washington, DC: American Psychological Association.

Pennebaker, James W. 1990. *Opening Up: The Healing Power of Confiding in Others*. New York: Avon Books.

Pennebaker, James W. 2004. *Writing to Heal: A Guided Journal for Recovering from Trauma and Emotional Upheaval*. Oakland, CA: New Harbinger Publications.

Pennebaker, James W., ed. 1995. *Emotion, Disclosure, & Health*. Washington, DC: American Psychological Association.

Philips, Deborah, Liz Linington, and Debra Penman. 1999. *Writing Well: Creative Writing and Mental Health*. Philadelphia: Jessica Kingsley Publishers.

Zimmerman, Susan. 2002. *Writing to Heal the Soul*. New York: Three Rivers Press.

**Internet Resources**

www.theawakeningsproject.org—The Awakenings Project. Publishes an annual literary journal, *The Awakenings Review*, written by people with mental illness.

www.psy.utexas.edu/Pennebaker—The website of James W. Pennebaker, a leading researcher in writing and health. Includes research summaries, online surveys and research to participate in, and extensive original scientific references.

## GENERAL WRITING ADVICE AND TECHNIQUE

### Books

Bennett, Hal Zina. 1995. *Write from the Heart: Unleashing the Power of Your Creativity*. Novato, CA: Nataraj.

Brogan, Kathryn S. 2006. *Writer's Market*. Cincinnati, OH: Writer's Digest Books.

Conroy, Frank, ed. 1999. *The Eleventh Draft: Craft and the Writing Life from the Iowa Writers' Workshop*. New York: HarperCollins.

Dillard, Annie. 1989. *The Writing Life*. New York: Harper & Row.

Goldberg, Bonnie. 1996. *Room to Write: Daily Invitations to a Writer's Life*. New York: Tarcher/Putnam.

Goldberg, Natalie. 1986. *Writing Down the Bones*. Boston: Shambhala.

Goldberg, Natalie. 1990. *Wild Mind: Living the Writer's Life*. New York: Bantam.

Joselow, Beth Baruch. 1995. *Writing without the Muse: 50 Beginning Exercises for the Creative Writer*. Brownsville, OR: Story Line Press.

Lamott, Anne. 1994. *Bird by Bird: Some Instructions on Writing and Life*. New York: Pantheon Books.

Ueland, Brenda. 1987. *If You Want to Write: A Book about Art, Independence and Spirit*. Saint Paul, MN: Graywolf Press.

### Internet Resources: General

www.writersdigest.com—The site of the magazine *Writer's Digest*. Packed with prompts, online workshops, book clubs, tips, contests, conference information, book information, and the magazine's "101 Best Websites for Writers" list. A good place to start exploring the enormous online world of writing.

## Internet Resources: Prompts

www.creativewritingprompts.com—Includes more than three hundred writing prompts and ideas.

www.dragonwritingprompts.blogsome.com—Hundreds of writing prompts, separated into categories.

writeoutofdepression.blogspot.com—The author's blog with writing prompts and other resources.

## Internet Resources: To Post Your Writing Online

www.authornation.com—Create a portfolio of your writing, build a network of peers to give support or feedback, join discussion forums.

www.blogger.com—One place to start your blog. Easy instructions.

www.editred.com—Get peer critiques, publishing tips, connections with publishers.

www.writing.com—Store and display your writing portfolio, writing tools, forums.

# JOURNALING

## Books

Adams, Kathleen. 1990. *Journal to the Self: Twenty-Two Paths to Personal Growth*. New York: Warner Books.

Adams, Kathleen. 1998. *The Way of the Journal: A Journal Therapy Workbook for Healing*. Baltimore, MD: The Sidran Institute Press.

Baldwin, Christina. 1977. *One to One: Self-Understanding through Journal Writing*. New York: M. Evans and Company.

Baldwin, Christina. 1991. *Life's Companion: Journal Writing as a Spiritual Quest*. New York: Bantam.

Weldon, Michele. 2001. *Writing to Save Your Life: How to Honor Your Story through Journaling*. Center City, MN: Hazelden.

## Internet Resources

www.journaltherapy.com—The Center for Journal Therapy. Journaling instructor Kathleen Adams's organization for using journaling to heal; includes resources, suggestions, links.

## POETRY

### Books

Addonizio, Kim, and Dorianne Laux. 1997. *The Poet's Companion: A Guide to the Pleasures of Writing Poetry*. New York: W. W. Norton & Company.

Fox, John. 1997. *Poetic Medicine: The Healing Art of Poem-Making*. New York: Tarcher/Putnam.

Kooser, Ted. 2005. *The Poetry Home Repair Manual: Practical Advice for Beginning Poets*. Lincoln, NE: University of Nebraska Press.

Mazza, Nicholas. 2003. *Poetry Therapy: Theory and Practice*. New York: Brunner-Routledge.

Oliver, Mary. 1994. *A Poetry Handbook: A Prose Guide to Understanding and Writing Poetry*. New York: Harcourt.

### Internet Resources

www.poetrypoetry.com—An audio poetry site including information, prompts, and links on everything "poetry." A good place to start exploring.

www.poetrytherapy.org—National Association for Poetry Therapy. Information and resources on using poetry and other literature for healing.

## MEMOIR—INSTRUCTION AND EXAMPLES

### Books

Aftel, Mandy. 1996. *The Story of Your Life: Becoming the Author of Your Experience*. New York: Simon & Schuster.

Baldwin, Christina. 2005. *Storycatcher: Making Sense of Our Lives through the Power and Practice of Story*. Novato, CA: New World Library.

Barrington, Judith. 2002. *Writing the Memoir: From Truth to Art*. Portland, OR: The Eighth Mountain Press.

Freedom Writers, with Erin Gruwell. 1999. *The Freedom Writers Diary*. New York: Broadway Books.

Jamison, Kay Redfield. 1995. *An Unquiet Mind: A Memoir of Moods and Madness*. New York: Alfred A. Knopf.

Manning, Marsha. 1994. *Undercurrents: A Life Beneath the Surface*. San Francisco: HarperSanFrancisco.

Myers, Linda Joy. 2003. *Becoming Whole: Writing Your Healing Story*. San Diego: Silver Threads.

Rainer, Tristine. 1998. *Your Life as Story*. New York: Tarcher/Putnam.

Styron, William. 1990. *Darkness Visible: A Memoir of Madness*. New York: Random House.

Wakefield, Dan. 1990. *The Story of Your Life: Writing a Spiritual Autobiography*. Boston: Beacon Press.

Zinsser, William, ed. 1998. *Inventing the Truth: The Art and Craft of Memoir*. New York: Mariner Books.

## Internet Resources

www.storycatcher.net—The Storycatcher Network, directed by memoirist and teacher Christina Baldwin. Includes opportunities to contribute writing and many useful links.

www.storycircle.org—The Storycircle Network—Celebrating Women's Writing. Includes help in finding memoir-writing groups locally and online.

www.storyhelp.com—The Center for Autobiographic Studies, directed by memoirist and teacher Tristine Rainer. Includes help with finding local memoir-writing groups.

## FICTION WRITING

### Books

Alderson, Martha. 2004. *Blockbuster Plots: Pure and Simple*. Los Gatos, CA: Illusion Press.

Bell, James Scott. 2004. *Plot and Structure: Techniques and Exercises for Crafting a Plot That Grips Readers from Start to Finish*. Cincinnati, OH: Writer's Digest Books.

Bernays, Anne, and Pamela Painter. 1990. *What If? Writing Exercises for Fiction Writers*. New York: HarperCollins.

Frey, James N. 1987. *How to Write a Damn Good Novel*. New York: St. Martin's Press.

Kress, Nancy. 2005. *Characters, Emotion and Viewpoint: Techniques and Exercises for Crafting Dynamic Characters and Effective Viewpoints*. Cincinnati, OH: Writer's Digest Books.

Lukeman, Noah. 2000. *The First Five Pages: A Writer's Guide to Staying Out of the Rejection Pile*. New York: Fireside.

Lukeman, Noah. 2002. *The Plot Thickens: 8 Ways to Bring Fiction to Life*. New York: St. Martin's Griffin.

## Internet Resources

www.fictionfactor.com—*Fiction Factor,* the online magazine for fiction writers, includes articles, advice, interviews, online classes. A good starting point.

## DEVELOPING A WRITING GROUP

### Books

Reeves, Judy. 2002. *Writing Alone, Writing Together: A Guide for Writers and Writing Groups.* Novato, CA: New World Library.

Rosenthal, Lisa, ed. 2003. *The Writing Group Book: Creating and Sustaining a Successful Writing Group.* Chicago: Chicago Review Press.

Schneider, Pat. 2003. *Writing Alone and with Others.* New York: Oxford University Press.

## GENERAL CREATIVITY

### Books

Andreasen, Nancy D. 2005. *The Creating Brain: The Neuroscience of Genius.* New York: Dana Press.

Cameron, Julia. 1996. *The Vein of Gold: A Journey to Your Creative Heart.* New York: Tarcher/Putnam.

Cameron, Julia. 1998. *The Right to Write.* New York: Tarcher/Putnam.

Cameron, Julia, with Mark Bryan. 1992. *The Artist's Way: A Spiritual Path to Higher Creativity.* New York: Tarcher/Putnam.

Csikszentmihalyi, Mihaly. 1990. *Flow: The Psychology of Optimal Experience.* New York: HarperPerennial.

Sandblom, Philip. 1995. *Creativity and Disease: How Illness Affects Literature, Art and Music.* New York: Marion Boyars.

Wahlstrom, Ralph L. 2006. *The Tao of Writing.* Avon, MA: Adams Media.

## About the Author

ELIZABETH MAYNARD SCHAEFER is a trained scientist as well as a science writer, mental health advocate, and pioneer in using creative writing as a tool for easing depression. Since 1998 she has led a creative writing program for people with mood disorders that meets at the Stanford University Department of Psychiatry and Behavioral Sciences. This group draws members from across the San Francisco Bay Area and has been recommended by mental health care professionals.

Schaefer has lived through severe depression, and her knowledge and insight allow her to address the fears and concerns of people with this condition. She speaks on mental health issues, both personal and professional, to audiences including healthcare providers, police officers, community groups, and people with mental illness and their families.

She served as the West Coast Correspondent for *Nature*; has written on science and medicine for the Stanford News Service, *The San Jose Mercury News*, and other publications; and has contributed to science textbooks. Schaefer earned her Ph.D. in biological sciences at Stanford University.

# Index